101

Top Honeymoon Destinations

*The Guide to Perfect
Places for Passion*

ELIZABETH ARRIGHI BORSTING

ILLUSTRATED BY
KERREN BARBAS STECKLER

PETER PAUPER PRESS, INC.
WHITE PLAINS, NEW YORK

*For my husband, Kurt, who makes every day
feel as if we're still honeymooners, and for our
darling kids, Jake and Katie*

*Also for my Mom and Dad who, after
57 years of marriage, have proven that
the honeymoon can last a lifetime*

The publisher has made every effort to ensure that the content of this book was current at time of publication. It's always best, however, to confirm information before making final travel plans, since telephone numbers, Web sites, prices, hours of operation, and other facts are always subject to change. The publisher cannot accept responsibility for any consequences arising from the use of this book. We value your feedback and suggestions. Please write to: Editors, Peter Pauper Press, Inc., 202 Mamaroneck Avenue, Suite 400, White Plains, New York 10601-5376.

3 1232 00851 9011

Illustrations copyright © 2008 Kerren Barbas Steckler

Designed by Heather Zschock

Copyright © 2008
Peter Pauper Press, Inc.
202 Mamaroneck Avenue
White Plains, New York 10601
All rights reserved
ISBN 978-1-59359-801-3
Printed in Hong Kong
7 6 5 4 3 2 1

Visit us at www.peterpauper.com

MAY 0 7 2009

101
Top Honeymoon
Destinations

CONTENTS

INTRODUCTION

The best part of any wedding is the honeymoon. Don't believe us? Just ask any bride and groom. It's the very first trip you'll embark on together as husband and wife. And with seven continents, endless countries, and waves of oceans and seas, the most difficult part may be deciding where to go.

Ah, but not to worry. This book is designed not only to help you consider the endless possibilities, it's also intended to make the planning fun. We've divided the book into eight, interest-oriented chapters to help simplify the process. Do you see yourselves scouring museums and dining at the restaurants of celebrity chefs? Then you may want to earmark the *Cosmopolitan* chapter for some unforgettable urban getaways. Perhaps you want to visit several locations,

but still yearn for an all-inclusive, hassle-free sojourn. If so, then flip to the *Cruise* chapter featuring everything from cities afloat to intimate eight-passenger barges.

You'll also be privy to some well-known honeymoon hideaways, as

well as locations you may not have even considered: elegant all-inclusive resorts to far-flung places, luxe metropolitan hideaways, and some tried and true honeymoon havens. Not sure what to do once you arrive? Relax. We've also included a few romantic suggestions.

Yes, the honeymoon really is the *pièce de résistance* of any wedding. So, once the "I dos" have been said, the cake has been cut, and the bouquet tossed, it's time to make your escape to one of the *101 Top Honeymoon Destinations*. And let us be the very first to wish you congratulations!

Cosmopolitan

Happiness consists of living each day as if it were the first day of your honeymoon and the last day of your vacation.

AUTHOR UNKNOWN

Singapore

ASIA

Bubble Baths, Bumboats, and
Livin' Large at the Long Bar

THE BIG PICTURE

Step back in time to a more genteel way of living. A place where the sound of clicking mah-jongg tiles echoes from open windows, games of cricket are played on well-tended fields, and a "Singapore Sling" at the famed Long Bar tastes just as tangy today as it did when Charlie Chaplin would frequent this spotless paradise.

SPECIAL PLACES TO STAY

The 1887 **Raffles Hotel** *(T.1.800.768.9009, www.sing apore-raffles.raffles.com)* offers the quintessential Singapore stay for celebrating couples. Often touted as the best hotel in Asia, Raffles is all about old-world elegance and timeless style. History meets haute at the original Long Bar, birthplace of the celebrated Singapore Sling.

TOP ROMANTIC PASTIMES

- Kiss atop the Bridge of Double Beauty over Jurong Lake.

- Snuggle close, and embark on a bumboat ride down the Singapore River.

- Take a starry-night stroll through the fragrant Botanic Garden.

- Be ferried about in old-school style aboard a three-wheel trishaw.

London

GREAT BRITAIN

When It Comes to Romance,
London's Calling

THE BIG PICTURE

London certainly lures lovers, with its fog-laden weather giving couples ample cause to linger a bit longer in bed. Pull together your best Burberry ensemble and stroll hand-in-hand through the streets of London, where you're likely to encounter a bit of pomp and circumstance. There are picnic lunches at lush city parks, pints of lager begging to be shared at the corner pub, and quiet strolls along the Thames. When it comes to honeymoons, you'll discover London truly is a united kingdom.

SPECIAL PLACES TO STAY

A stay in central London can be pricey, but worth every cent. The city is divided into several boroughs, most of which are easily accessible via the Underground "tube" system. Located in the stylish Notting Hill neighborhood is the 24-room **Portobello Hotel** *(T. 44(0) 20.7727.2777, www.portobello hotel.co.uk)* which counts Gwyneth Paltrow and Colin Firth among its clientele. Rooms are all individually designed, from Moroccan themes to Zen-like abodes, each being romantically unique. For something a bit more traditional, nothing beats the five-star **Mandarin Oriental Hyde Park Hotel** *(T. 44(0) 20.7235.2000, www.mandarin oriental.com)*. This former Victorian gentleman's club is located across the street from Harvey Nichols department store and within a scone-toss of Harrods. Each floor has its own guest manager to ensure that each guest receives the personal attention they deserve.

The hotel's **_Celebration_** package is certainly kiss-worthy, with deluxe accommodations, freshly-picked rose petals strewn about, chocolate-dipped strawberries, a chilled bottle of Moët & Chandon Brut Impérial Rosé, hand-wrapped sterling silver earrings or cufflinks, dinner and champagne at the hotel's Michelin-starred restaurant, and a proper British breakfast overlooking Hyde Park.

TOP ROMANTIC PASTIMES

- Take the boat from Westminster Pier down the Thames to Greenwich, where you can share a kiss while one of you stands in the eastern hemisphere and the other stands in the western hemisphere at the Greenwich meridian.

- Take in a play in London's West End, where you can purchase tickets for half price at the discount booth in Leicester Square on the day of the performance.

- Enjoy afternoon tea on the grounds of historic Kensington Palace from 3 to 6 PM daily.

Paris
FRANCE

*From Eiffel to Eyeful, There's So Much to
See in the City of Lights*

THE BIG PICTURE

Dreaming of *la lune de miel* in Paris? Well, a Parisian honeymoon is without a doubt a monumental sojourn. For starters, consider the larger-than-life sights: Notre Dame, the Louvre, and, of course, *La Tour Eiffel*. France's capital city is also filled with beautiful gardens, dreamy sidewalk cafés, and charming neighborhoods, such as the artsy Montmartre. Every step brings a new discovery, whether it's a cramped bookstall with shelves of literary finds or the whoosh of an espresso machine beckoning from the river's edge. Share a seductive smooch—perhaps a French kiss—along the left bank. Ah, *c'est la vie!*

SPECIAL PLACES TO STAY

A distant and unexpected serenade by a talented street performer isn't so uncommon if you're nesting at the charming **Hôtel de Banville** *(T. 33 (0) 142.67.*

70.16, www.hotelbanville.fr). This intimate Art Deco hotel, located in a residential neighborhood not far from the Arc de Triomphe, houses just 38 rooms. Lovers are carried to their chambers in a tiny birdcage elevator. Request a room overlooking the rear courtyard and enjoy the ambiance from your Juliet-style balcony. The left bank **L'Hôtel** *(T. 33 (0) 1 44.41.99.00, www.l-hotel.com)*, where Oscar Wilde spent his final days, was built in 1816 and offers over-the-top luxury. Located in the heart of St-Germain-des-Prés, this sleek and sexy retreat offers 20 dramatic rooms built around a stunning oval atrium. *Très magnifique!*

TOP ROMANTIC PASTIMES

- Enjoy a night of naughty entertainment at the famed cabaret Moulin Rouge.

- Shop for French lingerie at Galeries Lafayette.

- Heat things up with a one-day cooking class at the famed Le Cordon Bleu.

San Francisco

CALIFORNIA

International Cuisines, Moving Landmarks,
and Incredible Bay Views

THE BIG PICTURE

Where else can you sup on sushi in the heart of Japantown, and then share a foam-laden cappuccino nearby in North Beach, the city's lively Italian neighborhood? And only the City by the Bay can offer lovers a ride on a moving landmark (the classic cable cars) and a chance to stroll arm-in-arm across one of the world's largest suspension bridges (Golden Gate Bridge). If you happen to be feeling completely carefree, take a topsy-turvy drive down Lombard Street, America's most crooked avenue, which winds its way from Hyde Street to Leavenworth Street.

SPECIAL PLACES TO STAY

As guests of **The Fairmont San Francisco** *(T. 415.772. 5000, www.fairmont.com/SanFrancisco)* you'll awake to the faint sounds of foghorns and the clang-clang of cable car bells. What a wonderful beginning to your

San Francisco day! Located atop tony Nob Hill, **The Fairmont** is a historic haunt, where the rooms are elegant and the service superb. Request the *Romantic Rendez-Vous* package, featuring two nights of luxury complete with rose petals and candles placed throughout your room upon arrival, a bottle of sparkling wine, and a candlelit dinner for two in the privacy of your guest room. Located near Union Square just a short stroll from the cable car line is the enchanting **Kensington Park Hotel** *(T. 800.553. 1900, www.kensingtonparkhotel.com)*. Affordable and alluring, this boutique hotel is incredibly charming, with spacious rooms, select city views, a convenient location, and complimentary tea and sherry each evening.

TOP ROMANTIC PASTIMES

- Nosh on sexy foods, such as fresh oysters, at the Ferry Building along the Embarcadero.

- Sip champagne and ponder the panoramic city views at the Top of the Mark, which sits on the 19th floor of the Mark Hopkins Hotel.

- Take a walk on the nude side of Baker Beach in the Golden Gate National Recreation Area.

New York City

NEW YORK

Carriage Rides and Cosmopolitans...
You'll Take Manhattan

THE BIG PICTURE

Is it coincidence that The Big Apple shares its name with the forbidden fruit? New York City can be decadent and decidedly wicked. After all, this is the city that never sleeps, and that's what makes it exciting. No matter what the hour, there is always something to enjoy: a horse-drawn carriage ride, a sultry cabaret show, or an award-winning Broadway play. Let's not forget the usual suspects as well: the Empire State Building, the Metropolitan Museum of Art, the Statue of Liberty and, at the top of every girl's list, a Holly Golightly moment at Tiffany & Co. A New York City sojourn is many things, but disappointing isn't one of them.

SPECIAL PLACES TO STAY

Snuggle up in front of an in-room wood-burning fireplace at the deluxe **Lowell Hotel** (*T. 212.838.1400,* *www.lowellhotel.com*). Located on a quiet, tree-lined street off Madison Avenue, this classic urban hide-away spoils its guests with thoughtful touches, such as complimentary beverages upon arrival, FIJI Water at turndown, and a selection of Bulgari bathroom amenities. Although honeymoons have little to do with sleep, you will experience a good rest at **The Benjamin** (*T. 212.715.2500, www.thebenjamin.com*). This elegant find employs a sleep concierge who will help you select from the hotel's pillow menu to ensure your stay is comfortable. Accommodations incorporate a blend of classic and modern designs with an array of services, such as in-room dining and massage, that seem tailored to newlyweds. Enjoy the *Champagne Dreams* package, which treats you and your loved one to chocolate-covered strawberries and a bottle of Veuve Clicquot Champagne to wash them down. Rose petal turndown and a 20 percent discount on a couples spa treatment are also included.

TOP ROMANTIC PASTIMES

- Ride in a horse-drawn carriage through Central Park.
- Honeymooning during the winter? Ice skate arm-in-arm at Rockefeller Center.
- Share a kiss at the top of the Empire State Building.

Hong Kong

ASIA

Dim Sum, and Then Some;
Hong Kong Is a Bona Fide Fantasy Island

THE BIG PICTURE

If you crave a sexy, sophisticated honeymoon with a hint of old-fashioned romance, then flee to Hong Kong for your very first tryst as husband and wife. Hop aboard a tiny wooden *sampan* where you can canoodle oh-so-close as you sway over a ripple of waves. Reveal your daring side aboard a thrilling roller coaster ride at Ocean Park, Hong Kong's lavish amusement park and marine education center. You can also share a lingering smooch at the park's Butterfly House as hundreds of free-flying inhabitants flutter above.

SPECIAL PLACES TO STAY

Wedded bliss begins at the elegant **Mandarin Oriental** *(T. 852.2522.0111, www.mandarinoriental.com)*. Incorporating the centuries-old practice of feng shui, the harmonious setting created behind your guest

room door serves to relax. Rich woods and elegant furnishings are displayed next to hi-tech gadgets. Water also plays an important role in creating balance, which is evident from the breathtaking views of Victoria Harbour—not to mention some sizable soaking tubs that can accommodate two! Every bride and groom can use a little pampering, and the **Hotel InterContinental Hong Kong** *(T. 800.327.0200, www.hongkong-ic.inter continental.com)* certainly knows how to spoil its guests. Five-star service runs the gamut from person-alized limousine tours to butler service. Rooms at this urban resort are luxe, and you can pick from one of three infinity spa pools to lounge by. If either of you needs to satisfy a craving for Cantonese food at 3 AM, simply place a late-night call to room service. Book the hotel's exclusive *The Suite Life* to enjoy luxurious Harborview Suites, round-trip airport limousine service, access to the hotel fitness club, full breakfast, afternoon tea, evening cocktails, and personalized concierge services.

TOP ROMANTIC PASTIMES

- See what the future holds with a his and her reading from one of the many fortune-tellers at Tin Hau Temple.

- Continue your jet-setting with a day trip across the bay at Macau, just an hour by jetfoil.

- Feeding one another is great foreplay. Set out on your own culinary tour of regional Chinese cuisine, and sample everything from spicy Hunan dishes to Beijing specialties.

Mexico City

MEXICO

Where Cosmopolitan and Colonial Collide

THE BIG PICTURE

Habla español? Even if you don't know the language, the scenery in Mexico City easily speaks for itself. You and your *esposo* will discover an ultra urban setting steeped in centuries-old history. Selecting such a cosmopolitan destination will show that the two of you are seasoned travelers who truly want to experience all the city has to offer. Spend your days, arms entwined, exploring the fabulous museums, public sculptures, murals, greenbelts, and plazas. Treat yourselves to a housewarming gift at one of the local markets or bazaars. If not something of heirloom quality, perhaps a bottle of top-shelf tequila?

SPECIAL PLACES TO STAY

In unfamiliar places, a recognizable hotel can bring peace of mind. Mexico City has a stunning, full-service **Four Seasons Resort** *(T. 52 (55)5230.1818, www.fourseasons. com/mexico)* that can easily make any newlywed feel pampered with its eight stories of opulence. The hotel, modeled after the 18th-century Iturbide Palace, offers romantic rooms with the best overlooking the interior courtyard and its trickling fountain. But if you want to stay in something a bit more daring, the pre-revolutionary-era **Gran Hotel Ciudad de Mexico** *(T.(55)1083.7700, www.granhotel ciudaddemexico.com.mx)* is a bolder choice. The Tiffany-crowned atrium, curved balustrades, and fanciful iron elevators recall an elegant epoch in Mexico's history. Rooms are rich in luxury with canopied beds and sitting areas, and the expansive rooftop beckons with its spectacular views and salt-rimmed margaritas.

TOP ROMANTIC PASTIMES

- Take a boat ride in a brightly-colored vessel along the canals—or "floating gardens"—and hire a mariachi band to serenade you en route.

- Relive the lives of Mexico's most celebrated couple—artists Diego Rivera and Frida Kahlo—and visit their home-turned-museum, Casa Azul.

- Stroll the cobbled streets of Coyoacan and San Angel, former villages that are now vibrant artist-filled squares.

- Get a charge by attending a bullfight at Plaza Mexico between November and March.

Buenos Aires

ARGENTINA

Midnight Meals and Sultry Tangos

THE BIG PICTURE

Buenos Aires isn't charming—it's downright sexy. This statement is easy to prove; just look for the nearest dance floor, where you can fuel your passion for each other while embraced in a tango. Don't plan on any early morning activities in this sultry city. Instead, you're in for late-night dinners, midnight tangos, and some toe-tapping jazz clubs which don't get started until around 2 AM. Your night on the town could easily end well after sunrise—just in time for mimosas!

SPECIAL PLACES TO STAY

File the **Faena Hotel + Universe** *(T.54.11.4010.9000, www.faenahotelanduniverse.com)*, located in the historic El Porteño Building, under one fabulous find. The Philippe Starck-designed retreat features 110 stylish rooms boasting modern elegance and a dash of decadence. The hotel is near the river and the

cobblestone streets of the San
Telmo neighborhood. Stretching
23 stories high with spectacular
views from the upper floor, the
Park Tower *(T. 54.11.4318.9100,*
www.starwoodhotels.com) is a
swanky, urban resort boasting
antique-filled rooms and many
perks, including an outdoor swimming pool where celebrities have

been known to lounge. Overlooking Plaza San
Martin, the hotel sits in the shadow of the Torre de
los Ingleses—the Buenos Aires answer to Big Ben.

TOP ROMANTIC PASTIMES

- Indulge in a sunset kiss on the Puente de las
  Mujeres ("The Bridge of Women") in the Puerto
  Madero.

- Few know that beef is considered an aphro-
  disiac. See for yourselves by sampling one of the
  city's many renowned steak houses for a satisfying
  meal.

- Go ahead, cry for Argentina from the balcony of
  the Casa Rosada, where Juan and Eva Peron
  dazzled their subjects.

Washington, D.C.
UNITED STATES

Life, Liberty, and the Pursuit of Happiness

THE BIG PICTURE

Honeymooning in the nation's capital can prove to be a lesson both in history and romance. In between visits to Capitol Hill and Pennsylvania Avenue, you'll find stolen moments along the Potomac River, C&O Canal and, in the spring, beneath one of the blossoming cherry trees. On warm days, flee to one of the city's well-tended parks for a lazy picnic lunch. Follow it up by renting some in-line skates to explore the park hand-in-hand.

SPECIAL PLACES TO STAY

Because of its storied history, which dates back to 1850, the **Willard InterContinental Washington** *(T. 202.628.9100, www.washington.intercontinental. com)* is one of the grandest hotels in the nation. Honeymooners enjoy elegant guest rooms with all the residential comforts of home, and just two blocks from the White House. If you have political aspirations (president and first lady or president and first husband), book the romantic **_Presidential Perks_** package. You'll slumber in the Thomas Jefferson Suite, and indulge in champagne, truffles, Godiva chocolates, dipped berries, round-trip limousine service from the airport, and both a champagne breakfast and three-course candlelight dinner over-looking the Washington Monument, served in-room. Younger newlyweds might want to stay in the college area of Georgetown at the six-story **Georgetown Inn** *(T. 888.587.2388, www.georgetowncollection.com)*, a boutique property located near the waterfront, shops, and restaurants. Former guests include royal roman-tics the Duke and Duchess of Windsor.

TOP ROMANTIC PASTIMES

- Sneak away to Georgetown's Dumbarton Oaks Gardens to share a kiss at Lovers' Lane Pool.

- Take a "Monuments by Moonlight" tour to view the city's treasures at twilight.

- If you're visiting in July, ooh and aah at the July 4th fireworks extravaganza from the National Mall.

Florence
ITALY

Where Art Imitates Life

THE BIG PICTURE

Maybe it's a little too soon to renew your vows, but
you can recite your recent promises to each other at
Palazzo Vecchio, one of Italy's best-known and most
romantic wedding sites, replete with billowy silk
drapes, crystal chandeliers, and gilded mirrors. This
medieval Gothic palace is located near one of the
city's greatest public spaces, the Piazza della Signoria,
where couples embrace both each other and the
many magnificent statues. Stroll the city—hands
clasped—and discover all the wonders Florence has
to offer: fabulous outdoor leather markets, famous
works of art, and a skyline of lofty domes that cast an
impressive silhouette at sunset.

SPECIAL PLACES TO STAY

Florence served as the backdrop for the film
A Room with a View, so you can expect to find especially dreamy rooms for your Florentine honeymoon.

Among the crème de la crème is the **Hotel Lungarno** *(T. 39.055.2726.4000, www.lungarnohotels.com)*, positioned alongside the Arno River. The luxurious private and public rooms, each reminiscent of a miniature palace, offer daring and dramatic settings. **Montebello Splendid** *(T. 39.055. 27471, www.hotel-florence-montebellosplendid.com)* certainly lives up to its moniker, with Tuscan-style loggias that open onto breathtaking gardens, a fountain featuring bronze cherubs, and a delightful neoclassic temple. Rooms and suites are deliciously decorated with bold fabrics and textures, plus romantic Juliet-style balconies. Complimentary breakfast buffet included. Consider this your introduction to *la dolce vita!*

TOP ROMANTIC PASTIMES

- Stroll the banks of the Arno by moonlight.
- Slip away to the Uffizi, and enjoy a frothy cappuccino from the museum's rooftop terrace.
- Enjoy a lingering walk through Boboli Gardens and take an afternoon wine break under one of the towering trees.
- Shop for some honeymoon bling from one of the stellar jewelry shops along the Ponte Vecchio.

Montreal

CANADA

Encounter European Élan in North America

THE BIG PICTURE

With its bilingual signs, frescoed buildings, and a certain *je ne sais quois*, it might be hard to tell at times whether you're honeymooning in Montreal or Paris. It's every bit as cosmopolitan as its European counterpart, with equally romantic nuances—cobblestone streets, sultry jazz clubs, and romantic waterways. So how kissable is Montreal, you ask? Well, consider this: Liz Taylor and Richard Burton were married in Montreal the first time around, and Céline Dion hosted her wedding of titanic proportions here, too. And, let's not forget about John and Yoko's infamous 1969 bed-in also held in Montreal. After all, as Lennon once sang, all you need is love.

SPECIAL PLACES TO STAY

Hôtel Nelligan *(T. 514.788.2040, www.hotelnelligan. com)* feels more like hip, loft living than the average hotel room. The pair of connecting historic buildings, dating back to the 1830s, features exposed brick walls and soaring ceilings. Guest rooms are luxurious, with large windows, romantic fireplaces, and double Jacuzzi tubs. Make a point to have an evening cocktail at Versus Bar in the hotel's open-air courtyard. With a reputation for having the largest bathrooms in town—including oversized tubs that can accommodate two—**Loews Hotel Vogue** (*T. 514.285.5555, www.loewshotels.com*) strikes a pose with its stylish interiors and central location. End the day with an *apéritif* at L'Opéra Bar, the hotel's two-story, glass-front lounge. Enjoy an indulgent escape with the *Romance à la Vogue*, which includes champagne and chocolate-covered strawberries; a three-course, in-room candlelight dinner; a selection of bath amenities; and breakfast in bed. Oh, *l'amour!*

TOP ROMANTIC PASTIMES

- Enjoy a starry midnight picnic atop Mount Royal.
- Linger in bed most of the morning with a breakfast of warm croissants and steaming lattes delivered to your room.
- Hire a horse-drawn carriage to ferry you through the city's cobblestone streets.
- Take a twirl on the dance floor aboard a slow-moving river cruise.

Bangkok

THAILAND

From Traditional to Trendy

THE BIG PICTURE

Amid the hustle and bustle of modern Bangkok, you'll discover a wealth of opportunities for romance. The mélange of culture and tradition leads to ancient temples and royal palaces, and includes some delightful surprises. Impress your new spouse with a bouquet of flowers from the floating flower market along the Chao Phraya River. Want to try something really sexy? Conduct a *9-1/2 Weeks*-style taste test with one of you blindfolded and the other playing the role of server. Hand-feed exotic Thai flavors, from spicy curries to pulpy limes to refreshing slices of coconut, to the masked participant. One night in Bangkok, and the world's your oyster.

SPECIAL PLACES TO STAY

Thailand is famous for its spa treatments, and few hotels have a better spa than **The Oriental Bangkok** *(T. 66. (2) 659.9000, www.mandarinoriental.com).*

The hotel's *Spa Indulgence* is ideal for honeymooners and includes a minimum of two nights in a deluxe room, American buffet breakfast, roundtrip limousine airport transfers, a his and her three-hour spa package, and a 4 PM checkout. Add to the mix the hotel's river-front location, excellent selection of restaurants, and impressive guest register of celebrities, and you're in for a memorable beginning. For an ultra-private get-away, stay in one of three traditional Thai villas at **Chakrabongse House** *(T. 02.622.3356)* along the river. Each abode features a balcony and breathtaking garden views, and a small footbridge connects the villas to the compound's swimming pool. Typical services don't exist, but the hotel's director ensures each stay is of four-star status.

TOP ROMANTIC PASTIMES

- Treat yourselves to a tour on the Chao Phraya River aboard a private longtail boat where you'll float past palaces, temples and out-of-the-way villages.

- Enjoy some together-pampering with a side-by-side Thai massage.

- Relive that first kiss while listening to *luk thung* music.

- Have a public "dining in bed" experience at the ultra swanky Bed Supperclub.

Istanbul
TURKEY

Where East Meets West

THE BIG PICTURE

Straddling two continents, Europe and Asia, Istanbul is a melting pot of influences. You'll be swept away by its fabled history, architectural treasures, and unencumbered beauty. Even with map in hand, it's easy to get disoriented, which makes for great romantic fodder. You may find yourselves meandering down cobbled alleyways unintentionally, only to discover something better than what you had thoughtfully planned—a footpath that leads to the channel, the aromatic lure of Turkish coffee brewing from a charming café, or a bustling bazaar filled with unexpected treasures. Spontaneity can often be a blessing in disguise.

SPECIAL PLACES TO STAY

Touted as the only luxury hotel on the shores of the Bosphorus, the **Çırağan Palace Kempinski** *(T. 90.212. 326.4646, www.kempinski.com)* was once the residence of the last Ottoman Sultan. The opulent hotel has been restored to its former glory, which is evident from the moment you cross the threshold. **The Hotel Empress Zoe** *(T. 90 (212) 518.25.04, www.emzoe.com)* is a less formal find, but unforgettable nonetheless. The inn is the marriage of several Turkish town homes bordering the ruins of a 15th-century Turkish bath house. There are 25 rooms in all, each with its own unique appointments, from Turkish textiles and Islamic folk art to French doors that push open to private terraces. You'll wake to the early morning call of prayer heard throughout the city.

TOP ROMANTIC PASTIMES

- Create a steamy scenario for just the two of you at a traditional Turkish bath, or *hammam*.

- Board the ferry to Princes' Islands and take a tandem bike ride tour.

- Take refuge on your hotel balcony after sundown to enjoy an illuminated and romantic skyline of mosques and minarets.

- Embark on an after-dark cruise down the Bosphorus with scenery of bobbing fishing boats and twinkling lights.

Adventure

And the honeymoon is just the beginning
of your life together. It should be fun,
and light, and a time for intimacy.

DIANE VON FURSTENBERG

Vail

COLORADO

Alpine Elegance Year Round

THE BIG PICTURE

Whether you arrive in the winter for some cross-country skiing or turn up after the spring thaw, you'll fall in love with all that Vail has to offer. It's fashioned after a charming European village, and together you'll wander the narrow streets, with their many galleries and upscale pubs.

SPECIAL PLACES TO STAY

Reminiscent of a Bavarian inn, the **Sonnenalp Resort** (*T. 866.284.4411, www.sonnenalp.com*) is a luxurious village retreat located just steps from the ski lifts, with cozy rooms, fine dining, and an indoor/outdoor riverside pool. At the base of Vail Mountain is the plush **Lodge at Vail** (*T. 970.476.5011, www.lodge atvail.rockresorts.com*), combining the elegance and charm of an alpine inn with the dining and amenities of a four-star hotel.

TOP ROMANTIC PASTIMES

- Hang on tight while rafting down the Colorado River.

- Take a carriage ride on a one-horse open sleigh.

- Have a snowshoe race across the mountain.

- Kiss beneath a covered bridge.

- Play with your food at a local fondue house.

Machu Picchu

PERU

Finding Each Other Near the Lost City

THE BIG PICTURE

Just like your recent wedding vows, Machu Picchu and the surrounding area are extremely sacred. Travel the ancient Inca Trail as a twosome, contemplating your adventure with each hallowed step. Cross the jagged ridge to the Lost City of Inca, and give

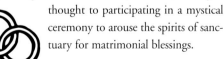

thought to participating in a mystical ceremony to arouse the spirits of sanctuary for matrimonial blessings.

SPECIAL PLACES TO STAY

A scenic three-hour train ride from Machu Picchu is the **Hotel Monasterio** *(T. 51.84.24.1777, www.monasterio.orient-express.com)*—a 300-year-old former monastery turned five-star sanctuary. Stay at the only hotel adjacent to the ancient citadel, **Machu Picchu Sanctuary Lodge** *(T. 511.610 8300, www.machupicchu.orient-express.com)*. Request a stunning mountain view room, where the two of you will want to spend an eternity.

TOP ROMANTIC PASTIMES

- Take a thermal bath for two in ancient waters.
- Learn to say "I love you" in the native Quechua language.
- Participate in a mystic ceremony with a shaman to fortify your love.

Sedona

ARIZONA

*Crimson Sunsets, Spa Retreats,
and a Dose of Spiritual Awakening*

THE BIG PICTURE

Perhaps the only thing that could possibly compete
with your post-wedding glow is the breathtaking red
rock landscape of Sedona. This desert oasis is the perfect spot to unwind, relax, and get in touch with each
other and nature. The morning sunrise signals a day
full of promises, while the burnished sunset is a
reminder—not that you need one—of how wonderful married life can be.

SPECIAL PLACES TO STAY

Take refuge in a canyon cottage at the luxurious
L'Auberge de Sedona *(T. 800.905.5745, www.lauberge.
com)*, rife with romantic opportunities. **Mii Amo
Destination Spa at Enchantment** *(T. 888.749.2137,
www.miiamo.com)* is a destination within a resort.
Sublime surroundings are found in the 16 spa *casitas*
and suites, where you'll be pampered beyond belief.

TOP ROMANTIC PASTIMES

- Hop on a tandem bike, and pedal along the back roads.
- Explore the hidden petroglyph sites.
- Count the falling stars at midnight.
- Have a spiritual reading to see what your futures hold.

Yosemite National Park
CENTRAL CALIFORNIA

Wonderfully Wide Open Spaces

THE BIG PICTURE

If the two of you treasure towering peaks, plunging valleys, and blue skies from dawn until dusk, you'll find you're in your element at Yosemite National Park. Explore the Southern Sierra and all its natural glory. Discover cascading waterfalls and towering walls of Ice Age granite. Where else can you admire such wondrous beauty, perhaps rivaling that of the person you came with?

SPECIAL PLACES TO STAY

The 1920s-era **Ahwahnee Hotel** *(T. 559.252.4848)* in Yosemite Village is a feast for the eyes with its imposing granite façade, striking beamed ceilings, enormous stone hearths, and tapestry of Native American artwork. Located near the entrance to the park is **Château du Sureau** *(T. 559.683-6860, www. elderberryhouse.com),* where you can book Honeymoon in Yosemite at this lavish retreat. Included are refreshments, dinner, champagne, herbal bath, breakfast, picnic lunch, and spa treatments.

TOP ROMANTIC PASTIMES

- Scale the cliffs together on a rock climb.
- Count the stars on a guided moonlight tour.
- Do a little snow tubing for two.
- Follow the trail of early pioneers on a mule ride.

Grand Canyon
ARIZONA

Back to Basics at the Historic El Tovar

THE BIG PICTURE

With few distractions besides the incredible beauty carved by rushing waters centuries ago, you'll really get to spend quality time together in one of the world's most majestic marvels. This great chasm offers a respite for couples following a whirlwind wedding. Take off, just the two of you, to roam the roads, hike the trails, or raft down the chopping currents of the Colorado River.

SPECIAL PLACES TO STAY

The three-story **El Tovar** *(T. 928.638.2631, www. grandcanyonlodges.com)* is a south rim institution. Opened at the turn of the 20th century, the inn was modeled after Europe's grand hunting lodges. The rooms are simple, but inviting. Savor a meal by candlelight in the El Tovar dining room where the best tables are those with views of the south rim.

TOP ROMANTIC PASTIMES

- Catch a falling star as you gaze across the night skies.

- All aboard—take a train ride on the Grand Canyon Railway.

- Pack a picnic lunch, and head for the marked nature walking trails.

Big Sky

MONTANA

At Home on the Range

THE BIG PICTURE

If you prefer stargazing to Starbucks, then you'll enjoy your moments together in Big Sky, Montana. Jeans and flannel shirts are the wardrobe of choice for fly-fishing, hiking and rafting. Still, there are days designed for cozying up in front of the fire. You can do as much or as little as you desire. After all, this is where the deer and the antelope play.

SPECIAL PLACES TO STAY

Enjoy a trouble-free trip at **Big EZ Lodge** *(T. 877. 244.3299, www.bigezlodge.com)*, where you can opt for the ***EZ Plan*** that includes all meals and on-site activities. Affordable elegance is found at the 29-room **River Rock Lodge** *(T. 866.995.4455, www. riverrocklodging.com)*, a classic ski lodge boasting complimentary breakfast, wet bars, and an outdoor hot tub. Reserve the Vista Suite with its double-sided fireplace.

TOP ROMANTIC PASTIMES

- Enjoy a movable feast with a moonlit sleigh ride dinner.

- Take a gondola ride high above the treetops.

- Witness the eruption of Yellowstone's Old Faithful.

- Race across the snow on a dogsled.

- Keep warm together while ice climbing.

The Big Island

HAWAIIAN ISLANDS

An Explosion of Scenery

THE BIG PICTURE

If the two of you are adventure seekers, you'll enjoy what the Big Island has in store. Conquer this scenic paradise together. Witness one of the most active volcanoes up close or hike the green valleys replete with towering waterfalls. Swim with the sea turtles, explore the jagged cliffs, and find time to take in those million-dollar Hawaiian sunsets each and every night.

SPECIAL PLACES TO STAY

Among the top of the tier for resorts along the Kohala Coast is the **Fairmont Orchid Hawaii** *(T. 808.885. 2000, wwwfairmont.com)*. Be pampered by the waterfront with luxe rooms, numerous restaurants, bars, golf and tennis opportunities, and beachfront cabanas. For a completely different

and more rustic experience, the 1900-era **Volcano Teapot Cottage** *(T. 808.967.7112, www. volcanoteapot.com)* is located in the cooler mountain region near the volcano. Its secluded location and vintage charm create a cozy hideaway.

TOP ROMANTIC PASTIMES

- Kiss in a lava tube at Volcanoes National Park.
- Swim beneath the waterfalls in deep natural pools.
- Hold hands while you snorkel through amazing gardens of coral.

Denali National Park

ALASKA

A Wild Time on the Tundra

THE BIG PICTURE

Words cannot describe the beauty of Denali National Park. From a distance you can enjoy such wild sights as grazing moose, grizzly bears, and caribou. The park is vast, the tundra untamed, and the geologic formations fascinating. Mount McKinley, the highest peak in North America, makes for a spectacular photo backdrop. Remember, a visit to Denali truly is a walk on the wild side.

SPECIAL PLACES TO STAY

Located within Denali State Park is **Mt. McKinley Princess Wilderness Lodge** *(T. 800.426.0500, www.princesslodges.com)*. Located on the banks of the Chulitna River, this retreat offers exceptional lodging and amenities. Eight miles from the park entrance is **Denali Cabins** *(T. 907.376.1992, www.denali-cabins.com)*, a cluster of 45 cedar cottages that are simple, but cozy, with free breakfast and outdoor hot tubs.

TOP ROMANTIC PASTIMES

- Go golfing at midnight during the summer when the sun still shines bright.
- Tour Mount McKinley by plane, with a thrilling glacier landing included.
- Ride in a covered wagon to a backcountry dinner feast.
- View the wildlife on a jet boat safari.
- Take a guided walk through the tundra.

Nicoya Penisula
COSTA RICA

Disconnect from the World
at Hotel Punta Islita

THE BIG PICTURE

If you fancy yourselves the modern-day
Tarzan and Jane, then you'll easily get
into the swing of things in this secluded paradise. Eco-tourism dominates these parts, and
you'll discover everything from nature reserves and
rural towns to some of the world's most powerful
surfing. If you seek adventure, both indoors and out,
Costa Rica can prove to be an exhilarating escapade.

SPECIAL PLACES TO STAY

Slip away to **Hotel Punta Islita** *(T. 011 (506) 231-6122,*
www.hotelpuntaislita.com), a secluded hilltop haven
overlooking the Pacific coast and featuring some of
the sexiest accommodations imaginable. Book the
four-day *Romantic Hideaway* package with daily breakfast, spa treatment for two, a torch-lit al fresco dinner,
and a selection of outdoor adventures.

TOP ROMANTIC PASTIMES

- Experience an adrenaline rush with a zip line canopy adventure through the treetops of the rain forest.

- Surf like pros in warm, wild waters.

- Explore the coastal and mountain roads behind the wheel of an all-terrain vehicle.

- Book a sensual massage for two complete with champagne toast.

Te Anau

NEW ZEALAND

A Slice of Heaven Here on Earth

THE BIG PICTURE

If you want to just let the world fade away so that you can have each other all to yourselves, let this South Island outpost make your wish come true. With nothing more than unobstructed views of Lake Te Anau, mountains, and farmland, you'll feel as if you've traveled to the end of the universe. Explore on foot (the area is touted as the "walking capital of the world"), horseback, or four-wheel farm bike. Who knew heaven was so close?

SPECIAL PLACES TO STAY

One look around **Takaro Peace Resort** *(T. 64.3. 249.0161, www.takarolodge.com)* and suddenly you'll be overcome with calmness. Each of the luxury chalets was designed by a feng shui master to help promote a sense of well-being. **The Fiordland Lodge** *(T. 64.3.249.7832, www.fiordland.co.nz)* mirrors its surroundings with wonderful views of Lake Te Anau and the national park. You'll find both lodge and log cabin accommodations private and secluded.

TOP ROMANTIC PASTIMES

- Arrange for a chef's picnic along the lake.

- Spend a quiet afternoon together fly fishing in one of 40 streams.

- Take a helicopter flight to the remote Milford Sound.

- Make the pilgrimage to Kawarau Bridge for an exhilarating bungee jump.

- Pamper yourselves with a 10-hand massage from a total of five masseurs.

Amboseli National Park

KENYA

Out of Africa

THE BIG PICTURE

Wake up each morning to herds of elephants wandering across the grass plains, lion cubs pouncing in the distance, and giraffes grazing nearby.  Amboseli boasts bright skies and breathtaking views of Mt. Kilimanjaro. After a day of exploring the terrain, make a stampede back to your digs and do a little pouncing of your own.

SPECIAL PLACES TO STAY

Rough it in style with your beloved at **Tortilis Camp** *(T. 254.20.603054.603090, www.tortiliscamp.com)* on the edge of Amboseli National Game Reserve, or at nearby **Campi Ya Kanzi** *(T. 254.45.622516, www. maasai.com)*. Both offer just a handful of luxury tents with wooden platforms, king-size beds, thatched roofs, expansive verandas, and full meal service.

TOP ROMANTIC PASTIMES

- Sip sundowners on top of Kitirua hill as the sun sets.
- Wake up early to watch the sun rise over the plains.
- Take a scenic flight for two over Kilimanjaro.
- Adorn yourselves with a piece of African jewelry made by local tribesmen.
- Sneak away to one of the nearby cliffs to do some elephant spotting below.

Fuji Lake Region

JAPAN

Nothing Lost in Translation

THE BIG PICTURE

Travel to the ends of the earth together in one of the most pristine regions to grace the globe—Fuji Five Lakes. These series of tranquil tarns sit at the base of Mt. Fuji, the famed dormant volcanic peak that erupts with eternal beauty. Lake Kawaguchi, the most accessible of lakes, is an oversized playground for enjoying outdoor activities. During the spring you and your sweetheart can witness the explosion of cherry blossoms along the north shore.

SPECIAL PLACES TO STAY

Combine your visit to the Fuji Five Lakes region by camping in **Fuji-Hakone-Izu National Park** *(Contact Yumoto Tourist Office: T. 0460.5.8911)*, which touches the sky at nearly 13,000 feet, and enjoying a more civilized stay at **Fuji View Hotel** *(T. 81.555.83.2211, www.fujiview.jp)* on the shores of Lake Kawaguchi. Forgo the Western-style accommodations, opting for a traditional Japanese room. Forget your jammies? Not to worry; the hotel provides guests with a *yukata* (Japanese loungewear).

TOP ROMANTIC PASTIMES

- Warm each other up while exploring an ice cave.

- Get naked at a private *ryokan* and enjoy a hot-spring bath together.

- Purchase a *bento* box (Japanese-style picnic) and have your lunch at the base of Mt. Fuji.

- Feed each other *hoto* noodles using chopsticks.

- Enjoy a *sake* sunset toast on the banks of the lake.

Alberta

CANADA

A Romantic Rocky Mountain High

THE BIG PICTURE

Become one with nature and be naturally pampered among the rugged peaks of the Canadian Rockies. The region is virtually untouched by man save for a few populated regions. Lounge lakeside at a rustically refined resort or explore the wilderness of Canada's national park system. Following a steamy night, chill out with a drive along incredible Icefields Parkway, named for its glacier scenery.

SPECIAL PLACES TO STAY

Located on its own island in Yoho National Park is the hand-hewn timbered **Emerald Lake Lodge** *(T. 250.343.6321, www.emeraldlake lodge.com)*. Strewn across the terrain are two dozen newly built cabin-style buildings outfitted with balconies, wood-burning fireplaces, and plump feather duvets. When money is no object, book the ***Diamonds Are Forever*** package at the historic castle-like **Fairmont Banff Springs Resort** *(T. 403.762.2211, www.fairmont.com)*. A few extravagances included: the presidential suite, his and her spa treatment, and a half-carat loose diamond.

TOP ROMANTIC PASTIMES

- Court each other all over again with a canoe ride on the lake.

- Have the chef prepare a picnic lunch to take on a hike.

- Stargaze from the bubbly waters of an outdoor Jacuzzi.

- Order chocolate fondue and a romantic comedy, and spend the night indoors.

Luxurious

And to sleep tight beside you,
listening to my silence within you
and your silence within me.

SAMUEL FEIJÓO

Napa Valley/Sonoma

NORTHERN CALIFORNIA

Eat, Drink, and Be Married

THE BIG PICTURE

California's Wine Country is an intoxicating place to honeymoon, and not just because it happens to be one of the world's leading wine producing regions. Motor along the wine trail in a vintage bench seat auto—sitting side by side—as you go in search of the perfect pinot noir.

SPECIAL PLACES TO STAY

When it comes to romantic places to stay, both Napa and Sonoma Counties have plenty of options. **The Kenwood Inn & Spa** *(T. 800.353.6966, www.kenwood*

inn.com) resembles a Tuscan villa with a cloistered courtyard, 29 romantic suites, a renowned spa, and a café and wine bar for guests. In St. Helena, you'll find **Meadowood Napa Valley** *(T. 800.458. 8080, www.mead owood.com)*, a luxurious, full-service resort situated on 250 acres of wooded land.

TOP ROMANTIC PASTIMES

- Embark on a movable feast aboard the elegant Napa Valley Wine Train.

- Get dirty with a side-by-side signature volcanic mud bath at Indian Springs in Calistoga.

- Take a personalized wine tour in a chauffeur-driven vintage Cadillac or Rolls Royce.

Scottsdale

ARIZONA

*Art Walks, Wine Making,
and Hot Desert Nights*

THE BIG PICTURE

Quench your thirst for fine living with an escape to Scottsdale, located in the sun-drenched Sonoran Desert. You'll have plenty of together time, whether it's lounging by a glistening pool or behind the door of your desert casita. Picture the two of you riding off into the sunset on horseback, and then moseying up to a western outpost for a plate of gourmet grub. The only thing hotter than the desert sun is the selection of posh resorts, dining options, and shopping opportunities that abound. Yes, Scottsdale certainly is a honeymoon oasis.

SPECIAL PLACES TO STAY

Spoil yourselves rotten with a sultry sojourn to the lavish **Phoenician** *(T. 480.941.8200, www.the phoenician.com).* With a championship golf course, a variety of swimming pools, 11 restaurants, and stellar service, you'll find little reason to venture far. The Phoenician is perhaps most spectacular at twilight, when the desert sky casts a crimson glow across the entire resort. Hang the "do not disturb" sign up for the *Grand Romance* package, featuring deluxe accommodations, a chilled bottle of champagne and fresh flowers upon arrival, plus breakfast delivered daily to your room. Although it's not technically in Scottsdale (the address is actually Phoenix), **Royal Palms Resort & Spa** *(T. 602.840.3610, www.royalpalmshotel.com)* is just a rose-petal toss across the city line. This is one of the very few hotels (if not the only hotel) that employs its own Director of Romance, who can create the ideal honeymoon paradise, from writing "I love you" in rose petals at turn-down service to arranging an astrology reading. Once you get a glimpse of the resort, though, you may feel you don't even need his services, as this place oozes romance with its cluster of casitas—many with their own private pools and fireplaces.

TOP ROMANTIC PASTIMES

- Head to a modern-day speakeasy, namely the Kazimierz World Wine Bar, with a secret rear entrance, nearly 3,000 wines by the glass, and live, smoky jazz.

- Listen up, brides. Enlist in a belly-dancing class at the Phoenician, and then show your groom what you've learned in private.

- Make and bottle your own wedding year vintage together at Su Vino Winery.

Orient-Express
ISTANBUL-BUCHAREST-BUDAPEST-VENICE

Relive the Days of a Bygone Era
Aboard a Moving Landmark

THE BIG PICTURE

Imagine a honeymoon in motion replete with elegant surroundings and ever-changing scenery, where a vintage bent seems to yield a gracious, more elegant era. Such is life aboard the classic **Venice-Simplon Orient-Express** *(T. 800.524.2420, www.orient-express.com)*. The six-day journey begins in Istanbul and travels on to Bulgaria, Romania, Budapest, Vienna, and finally Venice. Slip away to your luxurious compartment for an afternoon rendezvous or head to the famed bar car to sip cognac and watch the world drift by. Either way, your marriage is headed on the right track with such a storied beginning.

ON-BOARD ACCOMMODATIONS

Relive the elegance of 1920s Europe behind the door of your cozy carriage compartment, complete with wooden marquetry and original brass fittings. Unlike a static stay on land, you'll be assigned your very own cabin steward, who can be summoned by the bell in your compartment. You'll receive daily visits from the maître d', who will come by your compartment to take your lunch and dinner reservations. Breakfast, afternoon tea, and refreshments can be enjoyed in the privacy of your compartment. Fine dining is the order of the day as you and your darling feast on meals prepared by French chefs and served by Italian waiters on fine china and crystal. You'll also slumber overnight at the Athenee Palace Hilton Hotel while in Bucharest. Suite dreams!

TOP ROMANTIC PASTIMES

- Relive the romance of pre-war Europe with a visit to one of Bucharest's stately casinos, housed in century-old beaux arts palaces and casinos.

- Do some beautiful bathing *à deux* in Budapest along the Danube on the Buda bank at the 1570-era Kiraly Baths.

- Follow in the footsteps of Papa Hemingway with a visit to Harry's Bar, a legendary watering hole located across from the Cipriani Hotel in Venice. Sip dry martinis and sweet Bellinis, and drink in the views of Chiesa di Santa Maria della Salute from the second floor.

- Surprise your significant other with a trip to the bar car, where you've pre-arranged for the pianist to play your special song.

Dubai
UNITED ARAB EMIRATES

An Oasis of Luxury

THE BIG PICTURE

Dubai, one of the seven United Emirates, is like a Disneyland for adults. Where else can the two of you enjoy a camel ride through the arid desert one moment, then strap on some skis and glide down snow-covered slopes the next? Okay, so Dubai's ski resort is of the indoor variety, but you'd be hard-pressed to find anywhere else where you can go from bikini-clad to bundled up within minutes. While some marvels are man-made, those warm Arabian nights, coupled with days spent by azure seas, can only be credited to the kindness of Mother Nature.

SPECIAL PLACES TO STAY

Shaped like a billowing sail on its own man-made island, **Burj Al Arab** *(T. 971.4.301.7777, www.burj-al-arab.com)* is Dubai's premier, all-suite resort with water views from every room. You'll be spoiled by the amenities, as everything has been orchestrated to make you feel as if the two of you are the only guests to have checked in. Take advantage of the chauffeur-driven Rolls-Royce, discreet in-room check-in, private reception desks on all floors, and a brigade of trained butlers providing round-the-clock service. **The Royal Mirage,** *(T. 971.4.399.99.99, www.oneand onlyresorts.com),* a stylish resort along Jumeira Beach, is a compound of three distinctive, Moroccan-style palaces. Rooms run the gamut from luxurious suites to private, Arabian outfitted residences. The full-service resort will make you want to stay put, since every-thing you'll need and want is right on the premises: casual-to-elegant dining, sexy spa treatments, rooftop dining, and recreation. You'll feel like royalty at this very chic resort.

TOP ROMANTIC PASTIMES

- Partake in a desert safari replete with camels, belly dancers, henna designers, and falconers. End your adventure with a starlight barbecue of traditional Arabian fare.

- Pay a visit to the spice *souks* along the narrow alleys, and stock up on those known as aphrodisiacs.

- Embark on an exotic cruise along the Dubai Creek or Gulf in a traditional wooden *dhow*.

- Toast at the top of the Burj-Al-Arab resort in the Skyview Bar, then enlist the resident mixologist to create a honeymoon drink in your honor.

Queen Mary 2

TRANSATLANTIC CROSSING: SOUTHAMPTON TO N.Y.

A City Afloat

THE BIG PICTURE

Relive the era of transatlantic travel aboard this elegant modern-day ocean liner, the **Queen Mary 2**. Imagine you're the Duke and Duchess of Windsor employing an entourage of servants to carry aboard your steamer trunks containing ballroom gowns, strands of pearls, and perfectly pressed tux and tails. Bid farewell to Southampton, England, for a six-day Atlantic crossing to New York City. On board, recline on teak loungers, take part in a wine tasting class, or run laps around the Sports Deck. At night, sip martinis between sweeps across the dance floor, only to return to your stateroom in the wee hours to continue the celebration behind closed doors. Life at sea can be mighty grand.

ON-BOARD ACCOMMODATIONS

There are more than a thousand cabins aboard the stately **Queen Mary 2** *(T. 800.728.6273, www.cunard.com)*, from luxury staterooms to sublime suites, all of which provide a home base while at sea. Choose the amenities that are most important to you: private balcony, stocked bar, platters of canapés delivered on a whim, butler service, fresh flowers daily, pillow concierge service, or all of the above. Each stateroom offers lavish touches, from tasteful décor and rich wood furnishings to plush robes, slippers, and 24-hour room service. Stroll to your restaurant of choice—10 in all—visit the spa, enjoy a live performance of West End caliber, or take a gamble at the roulette table. Bottom line: you won't run out of things to do on this grand ship!

TOP ROMANTIC PASTIMES

- Sign up for a dance class and impress fellow passengers with your new waltz, tango, or samba moves.

- Get beamed up together at Illuminations, the ship's full-scale planetarium which offers courses in celestial navigation.

- Indulge in a true British tradition of afternoon tea on the Promenade Deck. Feed each other fresh scones, clotted cream, and finger sandwiches, all delivered to you by white-gloved waiters.

- Book a sumptuous and relaxing couples massage at Canyon Ranch Spa on board.

Carmel-by-the-Sea
CALIFORNIA

California Dreamin'

THE BIG PICTURE

Go ahead. Make your day, not to mention an entire honeymoon at this charming seaside sanctuary. A favorite destination for both the famous and infamous—Clint Eastwood is a former mayor—the hamlet of Carmel looks as if it were plucked straight from the pages of a Grimm's fairy tale. Begin your day with a sandy stroll along the craggy shoreline, or sip a bowl of steaming espresso at one of the many charming cafes. Imagine evening walks by moonlight (most of the streets are devoid of lights), candlelit dinners at local bistros, and early nightcaps at a courtyard fire pit provided by one of the many local pubs.

SPECIAL PLACES TO STAY

What makes Carmel unique, and at times confusing, is that there are no addresses displayed on buildings. You also won't find a flicker of neon, national chains, or conventioneers—only charming accommodations such as the **Cypress Inn** *(T. 800.443.7443, www.cypress inn.com)*. This enchanting 1929 hideaway, owned by Doris Day, houses rooms in both the original structure and newly constructed wing. On the ground level is a charming lounge for afternoon tea, as well as an intimate bar where guests tend to congregate at night. Another great spot is the luxurious **Casa Palermo** *(T. 800.654.9300, www.pebblebeach.com)*. There are only two dozen spacious guest rooms and suites, making it feel as if you're staying at an estate rather than a hotel. Book the *Spa, Sea and Tee Escape*, featuring a spacious Courtyard Spa Suite, six 80-minute spa treatments, caddied rounds of golf for two on two golf courses, a pair of dinners at the Pebble Beach compound, and the use of a Lexus SC430 Convertible

Coupe, plus a his and her gift featuring two signature robes and golf shoe bags with amenities. "Fore" star service all the way!

TOP ROMANTIC PASTIMES

- Rent a tandem kayak and paddle to a secluded cove for a picnic.

- Take an afternoon drive down Highway 1 to Big Sur, and enjoy a romantic dinner overlooking the Pacific Ocean at the very exclusive Post Ranch Inn.

- Snuggle close and enjoy a classic film on the outdoor screen at the Forest Theater. Bring a blanket, gourmet picnic, bottle of wine, and enjoy the show . . . or not!

Santorini

CYCLADES ISLANDS, GREECE

The Many Colors of Island Living

THE BIG PICTURE

It doesn't take long to find an adventure in Santorini—actually, the adventure will find you. From the ferry terminal opt to take a mule up the steep incline to the top of the island which, according to legend, was formed by an eruption resulting in the lost city of Atlantis (believed by some to be beneath the water's surface just off the coast of Santorini). Once the two of you reach the top of this mythical island, you'll discover a terraced city of white-washed buildings, azure-domed roofs with doors to match, and beaches blanketed in black sand. This is the rainbow of unconventional colors you'll find on the island of Santorini.

SPECIAL PLACES TO STAY

Situated on the island's breathtaking Oia cliffs, the five-star **Mystique Hotel** *(T. 30.22860.71114, www.mystique.gr)* certainly does possess a sense of magic. There are only 18 suites and villas, open May through November, offering sensational views of the sea and distant landscape. Every desire has been thoughtfully fulfilled by everything from oversized beds positioned to make the most of the dazzling views to a wine cave for traveling oenophiles. A cluster of 18th- and 19th-century homes form the **Aigialos Inn** *(T. 30.22860.25191.5, www.aigialos.gr),* an unbelievable island find in the capital of Fira. This quartet of honeymoon homes features marble floors, French doors leading to private terraces, some with

their own swimming pools, and views of the caldera. The inn includes its own resident-only restaurant. Of course, you can always bring the feast back to your abode and enjoy it in private.

TOP ROMANTIC PASTIMES

- Sample some of Santorini's wine during a tasting at one of the island's vineyards, which happens to be a favorite site for local weddings.

- If you're feeling uninhibited, find a secluded spot on the beach and sunbathe *au naturel*—it's common *and* legal!

- Take an afternoon to explore the villages and their narrow cobblestone paths, prowl the local shops, and find a table for two at a local café for lunch.

- Charter a sailboat, and enjoy a sunset cruise on the azure waters of the Aegean Sea.

Tuscany and Umbria
ITALY

It Takes a Villa

THE BIG PICTURE

Bask under the Tuscan sun, as well as some spectacular rays in Umbria—two fabulously romantic regions in the middle of Italy. Both these Italian regions are known for their culinary contributions—so go ahead and dig for truffles, pluck plump grapes from the vine, and picnic amid olive groves, all the while feeding your euphoric mood, as well as your love for each other. You'll also get a taste for some tantalizing scenery: rolling hills, soaring cypress trees, vineyards as far as the eye can see, and ancient ruins in the more populated areas. Trysting in Tuscany, as well as Umbria, will result in oodles of amore!

SPECIAL PLACES TO STAY

If you crave hillside views and the aroma of ripened grapes, **Podere San Filippo** *(T. 39.055.8077995, www. san-filippo.com)*, set on 700 acres in the Chianti region of Tuscany, will certainly meet your expectations. Retreat to one of 12 luxury flats divided among a pair of newly restored farmhouse villas with vineyard views and occasional grazing deer. Sip *vino* (Chianti, no doubt) poolside, or taste test your culinary finds in the privacy of your kitchen. Enjoy a near religious experience in the Umbrian town of Perugia, where the two of you will slumber in the **Perugina Villa** *(Arrangements made through rentvillas. com, located in California, T. 800.726.6702, www. rentvillas.com)*, a lovely flat that was originally part of the Santa Maria Nuova cloister. Your two-story love shack includes a kitchen, working fireplace, and a small terrace overlooking the cloister's bell tower and rooftop. The abbey abode requires a minimum one-week rental; good thing there's no hurry.

TOP ROMANTIC PASTIMES

- Learn to make authentic Italian pizza in a hands-on cooking class, where the two of you can knead the dough into a work of art.

- Take a midnight soak at Cascate del Gorello outside of Saturnia, where hot, steamy water cascades over terraced limestone, offering million-dollar views of the Tuscan countryside.

- Share a passionate kiss—Italian style—on the medieval pedestrian bridge Il Ponte della Maddalena near Lucca, where you're likely to fall in love with the stunning views.

Santa Barbara

CALIFORNIA

The American Riviera

THE BIG PICTURE

Santa Barbara attracts plenty of celebrity visitors, but this red-tiled town is completely devoid of tinsel. Its enviable climate, velvety sand beaches, charming shopping district, and award-winning wine region are the stuff honeymoons are made of. Spend your afternoons gazing across the table at an enchanting sidewalk café. Evenings are best enjoyed along the waterfront or sipping margaritas at the end of a narrow Spanish-tiled arcade. Thankfully Santa Barbara rolls its sidewalks up early, so don't feel intimidated about hanging the "do not disturb" sign from your doorknob shortly after dinner. No one will know that you're not actually sleeping.

SPECIAL PLACES TO STAY

Tucked away on a leafy side street near downtown is the **Simpson House Inn** *(T. 800.963.7067, www.simp sonhouseinn.com)*, a luxurious bed and breakfast inn that will far exceed your expectations. Select your style of slumber: the main Victorian mansion, the original 1878 barn-cum-suites, or one of the free-standing, garden cottages set behind blooming flora and trickling fountains. Your stay includes a lavish breakfast and gourmet evening buffet accompanied by local wines. Follow in the footsteps of John and Jackie Kennedy by honeymooning at the storied **San Ysidro Ranch** *(T. 805.565. 1700, www.sanysidroranch.com)*, located in the foothills of Santa Barbara. There are 40 individually decorated cottages and bungalow suites scattered across the hillside and tree-lined paths. Book the **_Midnight in Montecito_** package, which pays homage to Vivien Leigh and Laurence Olivier, who exchanged vows in the wedding garden one minute past midnight in 1940. You'll retreat to a classic cottage, enjoy a chilled bottle of champagne, take part in an in-room couples massage, and receive $50 dining credit for breakfast to be delivered to your doorstep.

TOP ROMANTIC PASTIMES

- Travel the Santa Ynez Wine Trail, purchasing a dozen vintages with one to be opened each month on your wedding "anniversary" for the first year.

- Head to the bell tower atop the Mission-style Santa Barbara Courthouse for a million-dollar photo opportunity and a smooch above the mosaic of red-tile roofs.

- Get wild—on horseback, that is—with a western-style ride through the rolling hills of Santa Barbara.

Majorca
SPAIN

From Fiestas to Siestas

THE BIG PICTURE

Find yourselves adrift in the Mediterranean Sea on the Spanish island of Majorca, where warm days give way to hotter nights—metaphorically speaking. While the sun-soaked island is known for scantily-clad sunbathers and stylish travelers, it's anything but one-dimensional. Majorca is punctuated with rolling hills and tiny villages, which seem to have a calming effect if you prefer the road a bit less traveled. Sip sangria by moonlight, slip into your room in some historic inn, or romp in the surf from dawn until dusk. With so many options, is it any wonder that the Spaniards still enjoy their afternoon siesta?

SPECIAL PLACES TO STAY

Take refuge behind the doors of an 18th-century monastery situated in a picturesque island outpost. The 23-room **Son Brull Hotel & Spa** *(T. 34.971.53.53. 53, www.sonbrull.com)* is a minimalist masterpiece

containing streamlined rooms and suites with subtle hints of old-world charm. This haute hideaway offers as many services as any four-star resort: tranquil spa, *hammam*, swimming pool, a guest-only restaurant, and even cooking courses if you're so inclined. Nestled in the folds of the Sóller Mountains is the 12-room **Ca's Xorc** *(T. 34.971.63.82.80, www.casxorc. com)*. This luxury retreat sits behind 200-year-old walls of a former *finca* or farm. Each room offers its own unique touches, blending the traditions of island living with the decorative elements of Morocco. The original oil mill has been transformed into the hotel's restaurant, and the surrounding gardens and olive groves add to the fragrant ambiance.

TOP ROMANTIC PASTIMES

- Charter a boat and moor beside one of the sheer cliffs to enjoy a picnic afloat.

- Enjoy some outdoor aromatherapy with a leisurely and leafy walk through the fragrant orange and olive groves.

- Visit the lovely Carthusian Monastery with its stunning gardens, cloisters, and pre-paparazzi scandal: This is where Frederic Chopin and

George Sand wintered together in 1838.

- Take part in an island fiesta, such as Sant Joan, on June 23, which celebrates the arrival of summer with beach bonfires, fireworks, and devil-clad islanders.

- Spend an evening sampling tapas and sangria at a cozy sidewalk café.

- Learn how to flamenco like a pro, and display your moves in private.

Paphos

THE ISLAND OF CYPRUS

One Country, Two Cultures

THE BIG PICTURE

Play the roles of Greek god and goddess on this idyllic Mediterranean island, the birthplace of Aphrodite—the goddess of fertility, love, and beauty. Once ruled by Greeks, Turks, and the British, and conquered by countless other countries throughout the centuries, Cyprus finally gained its independence in 1960. Greek and Turkish influences still remain strong, so at times it may feel as if you're in two different countries simultaneously. The charming town of Paphos, where a few of the finer resorts are found, is where the two of you can quietly stroll along the waterfront, slipping inside a cozy taverna to enjoy a meal by candlelight. If you're planning on a winter honeymoon, pack both your boots and bikini. You can race each other on skis down the Troodos Mountains by dawn's early light, and then hit the soft, sandy beaches by early afternoon. And that's no myth!

SPECIAL PLACES TO STAY

Situated directly on the beach, **Almyra** *(T. 357. 26.888.700, www.almyra.com)* is a luxurious hotel with a crisp, contemporary feel, from the public spaces to those concealed behind doors. Many of the rooms feature jutting terraces with delightful views of the sea. The resort also offers an abundance of water sports, a pair of swimming pools, and a spa. You can also stroll to town from Almyra, and get a flavor for local living. **The Elysium** *(T. 357.26.844.444, www.elysium.com.cy),* located near the Tombs of the

Kings, is another stellar property featuring luxurious rooms, including villas with their own

private plunge pools. Retreat to the spa for a his and her treatment, or relax together in the Roman-style pool framed by romantic colonnades.

TOP ROMANTIC PASTIMES

- Visit the birthplace of Aphrodite, where legend has it that if you swim around the rising rock three times you'll both be blessed with eternal youth.

- Take a Jeep safari to the picturesque Akamas Peninsula, stopping along the way for fabulous photo opportunities.

- Do a little wine tasting at a historic Byzantine monastery.

- Shop for an original mosaic to remind you of your time spent together on Cyprus.

Exotic

Paradise is always where love dwells.

JEAN PAUL F. RICHTER

Turtle Island

FIJI, SOUTH PACIFIC

Be Pampered on a Castaway Island

THE BIG PICTURE

Fiji is a huge collection of tiny islands, but only a few are really honeymoon worthy. When your darling deserves only the best, flee to the private island resort of Turtle Island. Five-star and fabulous, this 500-acre paradise will make you fall in love all over again. The all-inclusive price tag also gives you the freedom to do as much or as little as you please.

SPECIAL PLACES TO STAY

Located on the famed Blue Lagoon in the Yasawa Island Group are **Turtle Island's** *(T. 800.255.4347, www.turtlefiji.com)* 14 *bures*, spacious thatched cottages on the beach. Lull your-  selves to sleep, entwined, on your veranda hammock. Have a special request? Your *bure* comes with a personal manager to help oversee those pesky little details.

TOP ROMANTIC PASTIMES

- Indulge in a side-by-side four-hand *Lomi Lomi* massage.

- Request a private picnic on the beach.

- Soak in your private, outdoor hot tub *au naturel*.

Dubrovnik

CROATIA

Marvelous, Medieval, and Mediterranean

THE BIG PICTURE

Popular with European honeymooners, yet barely a blip on the radar screens of their American counterparts, this classic Mediterranean destination offers plenty of romantic distractions. Take a cool plunge in the sea after dark, sip wine at a charming café, or marvel at the red-tiled roofs at dusk. Within the medieval walls are charming, car-free streets and narrow alleyways perfect for young explorers in love.

SPECIAL PLACES TO STAY

Situated behind the walled city is the 19-room **Puciç Palace** *(T. 385.20.324.826, www.thepucicpalace. com)*, an 18th-century marvel rich with gracious columns, arches, soaring ceilings, and antique furnishings. On a dramatic coastal bluff is the **Grand Villa Argentina** *(T. 385.20.440.555, www. gva.hr)*, a classic European hideaway with awning-draped windows and jutting balconies. Stay in style with one of their summer packages featuring dining by candlelight, four-hand massage, and sea view accommodations.

TOP ROMANTIC PASTIMES

- Take a ferry ride to nearby Lokrum to visit the hilltop fortress.

- Take a dive in the Adriatic Sea, one of the world's great diving destinations.

- Gather with locals in Old Town to observe the harbor by twilight.

Bora Bora

TAHITI, FRENCH POLYNESIA

Hedonistic Huts Strewn across the Water

THE BIG PICTURE

You probably are just coming off the high of having hosted a big, traditional wedding back home. Why not recite your vows for a second time on this romantic island? Dress in traditional island costumes, have the groom arrive in an outrigger canoe, and be serenaded by traditional Tahitian dancers and musicians on a white sandy  beach. As for the guest list, it's got two names on it— his and hers—and no one else. Now, isn't that romantic?

SPECIAL PLACES TO STAY

Drift off to sleep in a bungalow seemingly suspended over the water with glass-bottom floors, thatched roofs, seaside verandas, and full-service convenience.

Both **Le Méridien Bora Bora** *(T. 689.605151, www. starwoodhotels.com)* and **Bora Bora Nui Resort and Spa** *(T. 689.603300, www.starwoodhotels.com)* offer such extravagances on the most intimate sojourn of your lives.

TOP ROMANTIC PASTIMES

- Have the chef prepare you a romantic dinner to enjoy on your veranda.
- Hold hands—and your breath—to swim with the turtles.
- Take a sunset ride in a traditional dugout canoe.
- Spend some time together on a tandem raft drifting on the lagoon.

Marrakech

MOROCCO

Rock the Kasbah

THE BIG PICTURE

If you're curious about what the future holds, you can always enlist the help of one of the many snake charmers or fortune-tellers known to set up shop in Marrakech's Djemaa el-Fna Square. Better yet, leave fate to chance and, instead, take a magic carpet ride—metaphorically speaking—to the exotic *souks*, spice markets, and chatty bazaars in search of some bridal bling.

SPECIAL PLACES TO STAY

With just seven sultry rooms, **Riad Kniza** *(T. 212.24.37.69.42, www.riadkniza.com)* is a romantically charming inn hailing from the 18th century. Located in the heart of the old medina of Marrakech, this intimate hideaway is ideal for honeymooners in search of some serious seclusion, yet it's close to all the city treasures. **Riyad al Moussika** *(T. 212 (0) 24.38. 90.67, www.riyad-al-moussika.com)* is a former palace with just a half-dozen rooms under one storied roof. There is an Andalusian-style pool, music room, and a traditional steam bath. Slip away to the rooftop terraces to sunbathe or feast by candlelight.

TOP ROMANTIC PASTIMES

- Take a crash course in Arabic calligraphy and pen a love note to your beloved.

- Enjoy a ride in a *calèche*, a canopied horse-drawn carriage.

- Learn to make perfect couscous at one of Marrakech's many culinary schools.

- Hang with the locals on a terrace on Djemaa el Fna, where you can enjoy a cool beverage and drink in the views of the town square.

Nha Trang

VIETNAM

Once upon a Time in a Land Far, Far Away

THE BIG PICTURE

Bask in the beauty of Southeast Asia, where skies are an enviable shade of blue and the sea is as warm as bath water. Nha Trang is Vietnam's premier coastal community, with velvety sands and French influences. While you'll find traces of western culture, break out of your comfort zones to sample the regional fare, such as *gio lua* or *nem ran*. As for what to pack, let's put it this way—no shirt, no shoes, no problem.

SPECIAL PLACES TO STAY

Evason Hideaway & Six Senses Spa at Ana Mandara *(T. 84.58.524.268, www.sixsenses.com)* is a lesson in luxury. The collection of rustic villas has a far-flung feel coupled with all the extravagances imaginable. Your very own plunge pool and direct access to the beach add to its allure.

TOP ROMANTIC PASTIMES

- Spend the day at the beach beneath an umbrella designed for two.
- Explore the local villages, the markets, and the friendly people.
- Go for a long, leisurely sunrise mountain walk.
- Go island hopping to nearby Hon Rom, Hon Mot, or Hon Mun.
- Enroll in dive school, and explore Nha Trang from below the water's surface.

Phuket
THAILAND

Flee to the Far Reaches of the Earth

THE BIG PICTURE

The two of you will enjoy the scenery below the water as much as above. That's because Phuket's underwater seascape is teeming with coral reefs, countless marine wonders, and several varieties of sea turtles. Grab your bikini and trunks, and see what creatures you encounter in the warm waters of the Andaman Sea.

SPECIAL PLACES TO STAY

A wave of serenity prevails at **Banyan Tree Phuket** *(T. 66.76.324.374, www.banyantree.com)*, a haven bordered by golden sands and gentle waves. Overlooking Bang Tao Bay, your private pool villa offers tranquility and elegance. Ask for the *Heavenly Honeymoon* package for some added amenities and pampering. Leave your cares behind atop Surin Hill overlooking the Andaman Sea at **Treetops Arasia** *(T. 66.76.271. 271, www.treetops-arasia.com)*, a traditional Thai resort with sexy suites, private gardens, lotus ponds, and in-room infinity-edge pools.

TOP ROMANTIC PASTIMES

- Lather up together behind the door of your al fresco shower.
- Go scuba diving or snorkeling for some underwater beauty.
- Share a candlelit dinner on the beach.
- Celebrate the colorful Loy Kratong, held on full moon night in November.

Riviera Maya

YUCATAN PENINSULA, MEXICO

Relaxing in the Shadow of Ancient Ruins

THE BIG PICTURE

You may have plans for starting a family, but that doesn't mean you yearn to hear the pitter patter of little feet on your honeymoon. Riviera Maya is ideal for newlyweds because the region caters to couples traveling without children. No sand toys strewn on the beach, no tantrums in public spaces, and no menus listing chicken fingers. Instead, you'll find hand-holding, tender caresses, and long, lingering kisses by consenting adults.

SPECIAL PLACES TO STAY

Both Ceiba del Mar *(T. 52.998.872.80.60, www. ceibadelmar.com)* and **Maroma** *(T. 52.998.872.80.00, www.maromahotel.com)* cater to adults only, which makes them ideal for traveling twosomes. Each offers lavish accommodations, spa sanctuaries, elegant dining, and a full range of resort amenities. Each resort features a honeymoon package, too, including daily meals, spa treaments, luxe accommodations, and other great perks.

TOP ROMANTIC PASTIMES

- Journey to a forgotten civilization with a day trip to the pyramids.

- Go wild with a tour into the Mayan jungle.

- Take a dive with the dolphins for an unforgettable experience.

- Participate in an archeological dig, and see who finds a treasure first.

Corfu

GREECE

Unique Pairings of Pasta and Cricket

THE BIG PICTURE

This picturesque Ionian island, with Venetian, British and, of course, Greek influences, will have you falling in love all over again. Calm seas, tiny villages, and alabaster dwellings that hug the hillside all have a dreamy quality. Imagine casting a line from a traditional fishing boat on some secluded bay or strolling along the water's edge by moonlight.

SPECIAL PLACES TO STAY

Hidden within a private olive grove on the beach of Agios Ioannis Peristeron, **Marbella Corfu** *(T. 30. 26610.71183.8, www.marbella.gr)* is an exceptional island retreat with a collection of rooms overlooking the cobalt waters of the Mediterranean. Full-service amenities abound, including a collection of resort restaurants. The rooms at **Hotel Ermones Golf Palace** *(T. 30.26610.94045, www.corfu-hotelsermonesgolf.gr)*

are comfortable and roomy, but it's the incredible location and water views which earn high marks.

TOP ROMANTIC PASTIMES

- Sample kumquat liqueur, a Corfu staple since the late 1800s.
- Commission a pottery artist to create a custom-made address plaque with your names.
- Have a smashing good time at the annual Easter Pot Smashing, where breakables are smashed on the sidewalk.
- Sip wine and watch a cricket game along the Esplanade.

A Sojourn of Monumental Proportions

THE BIG PICTURE

Take in the exotic scents of Agra, a heady combination of jasmine, honeysuckle, and sandalwood, as you wander the bazaars and palaces of this wondrous city.

Standing as a towering symbol of love is the Taj Mahal, the seventh wonder of the world. A trip to Agra is certainly befitting for a rajah and his princess bride.

SPECIAL PLACES TO STAY

Enjoy a front row view of the Taj Mahal at the opulent **Oberoi Amarvilas** *(T. 91.562.223.1515, www.oberoihotels.com),* featuring Moorish-inspired rooms, ornate fountains, and impeccable five-star service. The modern **Taj View Hotel** *(T. 866.969.1.825, www.tajhotels.com)* also stands in the shadow of the great monument and offers nicely-appointed rooms and suites plus an array of amenities.

TOP ROMANTIC PASTIMES

- Have your recent nuptials blessed at a Shiva Temple.

- Awaken early to witness the beauty of the Taj Mahal at dawn's first light.

- Tour the countryside in tandem by elephant.

- Learn how to make exotic Indian dishes at a local culinary school.

- Get in on a game of cricket, one of India's all-time favorite sports.

Siem Reap

CAMBODIA

A Collage of Cultural Wonders

THE BIG PICTURE

You've plotted and planned your ideal honeymoon, and now you've arrived at the cultural capital of Cambodia. Set out together to enjoy this once-in-a-lifetime experience, exploring the ancient architectural wonder of the Angkor Wat temple compound. Your days will be busy and fulfilling as you explore Siem Reap from dawn until dusk. At night, retreat to your own temple—the one that comes with its own "do not disturb" sign.

SPECIAL PLACES TO STAY

Nest in the former digs of King Norodom Sihanouk at the unbelievable **Amansara** *(T. 855.63.760.333, www.amanresorts.com)*, featuring a dozen spacious rooms with many boasting private pools. Touted as the hotel closest to the ruins of Angkor Wat, **Sofitel Royal Angkor** *(T. 855. 63.964600, www.sofitel.com)* combines French and Khmer influences that result in stunning accommodations coupled with a collection of restaurants and a lagoon-style pool.

TOP ROMANTIC PASTIMES

- Treat your feet to side-by-side peppermint foot scrubs.

- Fly in a helicopter to the Thai border temple of Preah Vihar.

- Grab a tandem bicycle and explore the city.

- Attend one of the many guest lectures on Cambodian history.

- Stroll arm-in-arm amidst the temple grounds of Angkor Wat.

Paradise Island
BAHAMAS

Lose Yourself in the Alluring Confines of Atlantis

THE BIG PICTURE

It seems like there are no limits to what you can do on Paradise Island—perhaps that's how it got its name. Take a dip with the dolphins, try your luck at the roulette table, or drape yourselves across a lounge chair on Cabbage Beach, one of the area's most breathtaking strands. Of course, you also have the option to order room service and play indoors. The opportunities are endless.

SPECIAL PLACES TO STAY

Atlantis *(T. 888.528.7155, www.atlantis.com)*, the island's sprawling full-service oceanfront compound, makes for an effortless honeymoon stay. Everything you need is on the premises. Book the ***Imperial Romance*** package, featuring Imperial Club concierge level accommodations, private limousine service to and from the airport, champagne and truffles, gourmet dining plan, a massage for two, and breakfast in bed plus more.

TOP ROMANTIC PASTIMES

- Unwind in spa robes inside a relaxation room at the Mandara Spa.
- Head to the resort's pottery studio, and mold together a keepsake creation.
- Set sail for a sunset cruise on a graceful catamaran.
- Play a game of strip poker in your room, and you'll both emerge winners.

Antigua
WEST INDIES

Your Island Paradise Awaits at Jumby Bay

THE BIG PICTURE

Say "I do" to this lovely island getaway. Wake up and take sail around the bay, head to the tennis courts for a friendly match, or go mallet-to-mallet on the croquet field. Slip behind the billowy curtains of a poolside cabana or spend the day visiting a neighboring island. In Antigua, you have the choice to do as much or as little as you want.

SPECIAL PLACES TO STAY

Forgo those all-inclusive, overcrowded honeymoon resorts, and stay at the plush **Jumby Bay** *(T. 268. 462.6000, www.jumbybayresort.com)* instead. Set on a

 300-acre private island just two miles off the coast of Antigua, the resort features a trio of platinum beaches and a collection of exquisite guest rooms and suites. Daily rates include all meals with unlimited open bar, afternoon tea, and many activities.

TOP ROMANTIC PASTIMES

- Gaze into each other's eyes during a private dinner on the beach.

- Have breakfast on your private terrace with rose petals scattered about.

- Indulge in an in-room Midnight Couples Massage by candlelight, complete with a drawn bath for two.

- Do a little smooching on the tiki torch-lit beach.

- Request a romantic turndown of candlelight, chilled champagne, and plump strawberries.

Punta Cana

DOMINICAN REPUBLIC

A Craving for the Caribbean

THE BIG PICTURE

If your image of the Caribbean is a postcard picture of swaying palm trees, white sandy beaches, dangling coconuts, and the silhouette of a hand-holding couple, then you'll find life imitating art in Punta Cana.

This tropical hideaway will have you frolicking in the cobalt waters, scrawling your names in the sand, and relaxing nonstop as any proper honeymoon couple should.

SPECIAL PLACES TO STAY

Cocoon yourselves inside a hedonistic honeymoon suite at the plush **Sivory Punta Cana** *(T. 809.552.0500, www.sivorypuntacana.com)*. Life is good with an ample-sized bed facing the ocean, in-suite Jacuzzi, wine cooler, expansive terrace, and much more. Request the ***Caribbean Romance*** package for even more kissable perks. Equally enticing is the **Puntacana Resort & Club** *(T. 809.959.2262, www.puntacana.com)*, offering a selection of rooms, suites, and beach casitas. The resort's Tortuga Bay features 50 suites housed in 15 deluxe villas. French doors swing open to admit cool ocean breezes, and the hotel staff will make you feel as if you're the only ones who matter.

TOP ROMANTIC PASTIMES

- Gallop on horseback through leafy palm groves.
- Crack open a coconut, and share the sweet chunks of meat.
- Enjoy a noontime soak in the "Fountain of Youth" at the Ecological Reserve.

- Visit a coffee plantation on a guided adventure safari.

- Embark on a kayak exploration on the open seas.

Cairo

EGYPT

An Oasis of Emblems and Icons

THE BIG PICTURE

You may think all roads lead to Rome, but Cairo is the center of all routes flowing to and from three continents: Asia, Africa, and Europe. Explore the city's mélange of traditional and contemporary architecture, visiting such icons as the pyramids, the citadel, and the tapestry of majestic mosques.

SPECIAL PLACES TO STAY

Located on the west bank of the Nile, the **Four Seasons Hotel Cairo at The First Residence** *(T. 800.819.5053, www.fourseasons.com)* offers impressive views of the great pyramids. Rooms are among the largest and most luxurious in the city. **The Sonesta**

Cairo Hotel & Casino (T. *800.766.3782, www. sonesta.com)* offers contemporary elegance, from the poolside bar and Turkish steam baths to the selection of spacious rooms and suites.

TOP ROMANTIC PASTIMES

- Take a romantic stroll along the Nile.
- Snap a honeymoon photo in front of the Great Sphinx of Giza.
- Enjoy a performance of Aïda under the stars, and in the shadow of the pyramids.
- Take a camel ride alongside the river's bank.

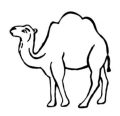

Cruise

*Once in a while, right in the middle of an
ordinary life, love gives us a fairy tale.*

AUTHOR UNKNOWN

Cruise on the Nile

ALEXANDER THE GREAT YACHT

Travel like Egyptian Royalty

THE BIG PICTURE

Get a taste for Egyptian extravagance on board the elegantly appointed **Alexander the Great Yacht**. Travel the exotic waterways paying visits to a plethora of ports, from Luxor to Edfu. Pack some thick eyeliner and a white designer sheet, and assume the roles of Antony and Cleopatra behind your stateroom door.

ON-BOARD ACCOMMODATIONS

Hunker down in one of 30 spacious suites decorated in colors and textures of the passing landscape. You'll find the level of service to be stellar with a gourmet restaurant, spa, Turkish bath, and mini gym. Request ***Executive Club*** accommodations for some added privileges, such as a private VIP lounge and all-day butler service. *(T. 202.579.4619, www.alexander-yacht.com)*

TOP ROMANTIC PASTIMES

- Enjoy a horse carriage ride to the temple of Edfu.

- Take a tandem camel ride in the shadows of the great pyramids.

- Fly high over Luxor in a hot air balloon coupled with a champagne toast.

Historic Burgundy Barge Cruise
FRENCH WATERWAYS

Raise Your Glass to Good Fortune

THE BIG PICTURE

Relax on the narrow canals of Burgundy, where you'll glide on the eight-passenger **Horizon II** luxury barge. This tranquil region features a labyrinth of waterways destined for a slow and leisurely sail. The two of you will disembark at quaint provinces to visit skilled vintners and savor elegant French dinners ashore. At night, you'll be lulled to sleep as you drift to your next destination.

ON-BOARD ACCOMMODATIONS

With only two levels and four suites, **Horizon II** has the feel of a private vessel. The attentive crew navigates an exceptional experience, from sumptuous cuisine and estate-bottled wine to open-bar privileges. Lounge on the sun deck getting lost in a tattered book or sip local wines while en route. *(T. 800.222.1236, www.fcwl.com)*

TOP ROMANTIC PASTIMES

- Sneak away among the grapevines for a romantic picnic.

- Eat local delicacies acquired from a roam around a lively farmers' market.

- Lounge on the deck at night watching fireworks in the distance.

Cruise the Galapagos
ABERCROMBIE & KENT

Erupting with Beauty Near the Equator

THE BIG PICTURE

The daily weather, water, and wildlife conditions will dictate how your time is spent on these volcanic islands. Days usually begin with a ride in a *panga*, a small rubber boat that ferries you from the ship to the island beaches. Get up close and personal with sun-bathing sea lions or snap a picture of lightfoot crabs scurrying atop the sand. It's a honeymoon with you, your beloved, and Mother Nature.

ON-BOARD ACCOMMODATIONS

Your high seas adventure takes place aboard **Eclipse**, a spacious vessel designed to negotiate inter-island landings with ease. Just 48 guests are housed in 27 spacious cabins all boasting porthole views. Meals are served in a single open seating, giving everyone an opportunity to compare notes about the day's events. (*T. 800.554.7016, www.abercrombiekent.com*)

TOP ROMANTIC PASTIMES

- Be each other's first mate while getting a lesson in navigation from the captain.

- Do some intimate midnight stargazing atop the observation deck.

- Take a hand-holding nature walk.

- After a long day of exploring, request a romantic candlelit dinner in your stateroom.

Monte Carlo to Rome

WINDSTAR CRUISES

Making the Most of the Mediterranean

THE BIG PICTURE

Clad in oversized sunglasses with attitude to match, you are following in the wake of Prince Rainier and Grace Kelly as you cruise the Mediterranean in style. You call on many wealthy ports along the French Riviera, including the fairy tale kingdom of Monte Carlo. Celebrate *la dolce vita* as you sail on to Italy and its many charming seaside destinations.

ON-BOARD ACCOMMODATIONS

It's the kind of vessel you imagine Aristotle Onassis and Jackie Kennedy sailed on, yet the eye-catching **Wind Surf**, with its billowing sails and extended bow, is *your* home on the open waters. The ship features a spa, lounge, and gourmet restaurant to help round out the extravagant experience. *(T. 800.258.7245, www.windstarcruises.com)*

TOP ROMANTIC PASTIMES

- Visit one of Europe's great perfume factories to concoct your very own his and her scents.

- Wine taste under the sun, spending a lazy afternoon among the vineyards.

- Step out in style to Monte Carlo's legendary casino.

- Stop at a gelato shop to taste every flavor they offer.

Alaskan Coast Cruise
REGENT SEVEN SEAS

Exploring the Final Frontier with Flair

THE BIG PICTURE

The two of you can huddle close to keep warm as you travel the Alaskan coast. The endless wildlife, from bald eagles and massive moose to spawning salmon, is abundant. The country club casual dress code makes it convenient for both of you to enjoy the environment in comfort, whether it's viewing bears in their habitat or marveling at jagged glaciers.

ON-BOARD ACCOMMODATIONS

Explore the great outdoors in style and comfort aboard the **Seven Seas Mariner**. This all-suite, all-balcony vessel boasts Le Cordon Bleu workshops, 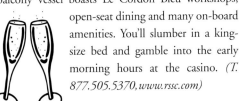 open-seat dining and many on-board amenities. You'll slumber in a king-size bed and gamble into the early morning hours at the casino. *(T. 877.505.5370, www.rssc.com)*

TOP ROMANTIC PASTIMES

- Take a tandem zip-line canopy ride through the treetops of the Alaskan forest.
- Catch a glimpse of Inspiration Point aboard a White Pass Scenic Railroad excursion.
- While cruising, be partners in learning the fine art of bridge.

Be Coddled in Croatia

THE BIG PICTURE

Once a playground for Roman Emperors, Croatia's Dalmatian Coast has emerged as a haven for honeymooners. Fall in love with the unexplored coastline, collection of islands, and romantic medieval towns which have yet to be spoiled by modern-day living. Once in port, you'll want to bike along coastal roads, explore Krka National Park and its stunning waterfalls on foot, or sample some of the Mediterranean fare served in the charming seaside bistros.

ON-BOARD ACCOMMODATIONS

The 30-passenger **Callisto** is a floating resort able to navigate the narrowest of waterways. Your state-room resembles a five-star honeymoon suite, and the two of you can make a grand splash into the warm waters of the Adriatic Sea from the swimming platform at the ship's stern. *(T. 866.551.9090, www. butterfield.com)*

TOP ROMANTIC PASTIMES

- Take out one of the ship's kayaks to explore a hidden cove.

- Feed each other exotic grilled octopus caught by local fishermen.

- Explore one of the quaint seaside villages on a tandem bike.

- Watch the submarine races on a secluded ocean bluff.

Singapore to Mumbai
CRYSTAL CRUISES

Exotic Asian Odyssey

THE BIG PICTURE

Cement your love at sea—five seas actually—on an exotic cruise from Singapore to Mumbai. You'll stop in ports rich in history with an edge of exoticness, such as those in Thailand and Myanmar. This is a voyage that begs to be different, and requires a bit of adventure and openness on your part.

ON-BOARD ACCOMMODATIONS

Slip inside your elegantly-appointed stateroom and push open the doors to your private veranda. It's time to celebrate at sea aboard the **Crystal Serenity**, a 1080-passenger luxury vessel boasting grand lounges, a casino, a pair of pools, and a feng shui-inspired spa. (*T. 866.446.6625, www.crystalcruises.com*)

TOP ROMANTIC PASTIMES

• Sneak up to the sun deck for a midnight stroll.

- Partake in a Buddhist tradition by walking around the Shwedagon Pagoda clockwise.

- Take a romantic cruise along the backwaters of Cochin.

- Act like a local, and take a ride around town in a horse cart while in Myanmar.

- Soak in the fabulous views of Chalong Bay from a different point of view—atop an elephant!

St. Petersburg to Moscow
VIKING RIVER CRUISES

Waterways of the Czars

THE BIG PICTURE

It's smooth sailing from here on out as you embark on a Russian river cruise. You'll journey to the country's two main cities, Moscow and St. Petersburg, marveling at all the manmade masterpieces, from the Kremlin to Red Square. But unlike a high seas adventure, you'll visit the smaller, culture-filled villages that hover along the less-traveled banks.

ON-BOARD ACCOMMODATIONS

With just 106 river view cabins on the **Viking Surkor**, you'll travel in comfort as you cruise along the placid rivers calling on lesser known hamlets. Scurry to the sun deck for a late afternoon snack, pay a visit to the sauna to let off some steam, and retreat to one of the restaurants whenever hunger strikes. *(T. 877.668.4546, www.vikingrivers.com)*

TOP ROMANTIC PASTIMES

- Take traditional Russian tea at a classic Moscow tearoom.

- Shop for some kitschy Russian nesting dolls to remember your trip by.

- Lounge together on the sun deck as you cruise the wondrous "Blue Route."

- Recite your vows, informally and alone, in front of an 18th-century church.

Barcelona to Lisbon
SEADREAM YACHT CLUB

Living Large at Sea

THE BIG PICTURE

Your Mediterranean voyage combines luxury and culture with a cutting-edge and romantic approach to adventure. You'll visit Gibraltar and Tangier in addition to Spanish ports.. Be active in Alicante or mellow in Málaga. Whatever you do, you'll be treated to first-class surroundings and sublime service.

ON-BOARD ACCOMMODATIONS

Board one of the two luxurious **SeaDream** yachts, and set sail in style. Leave the tux, tails, and ball gowns back home because the dress code is casually elegant and comfortable. Staterooms are ultra plush with cozy living room areas. Other perks include champagne and caviar canoodling, as well as double sun beds for snuggling on the open sea. *(T. 800.707.4911, www.seadreamyachtclub.com)*

TOP ROMANTIC PASTIMES

- In Alicante, race each other downhill on mountain bikes along the beautiful Costa Blanca.

- Enjoy a midnight meal of sangria and paella in the confines of your stateroom.

- Take a late evening walk to a local tapas bar.

- Explore your artsy sides with a visit to Picasso's birthplace in Málaga.

South America & The Amazon
SILVERSEA CRUISES

A Kaleidoscope of Exotic Scenery

THE BIG PICTURE

Satisfy your passion for adventure as you travel to lands of natural wonders. Unpack only once, but enjoy endless destinations, including Machu Picchu and the misty Amazon rainforest. Narrow waterways lead to surprising discoveries. Curious as to what that screeching sound might be? No worries, it's just howler monkeys high above wishing you a bon voyage.

ON-BOARD ACCOMMODATIONS

Consider Silversea's all-suite ship your home away from home. The vessel is large and roomy, yet agile enough to dock in more remote areas not typically visited by the masses. Your ocean view suite doubles as its own den of iniquity for some steamy stolen moments. *(T. 800.722.9955, www.silversea.com)*

TOP ROMANTIC PASTIMES

- Lounge on the deck and see who can spot the most wildlife while en route.

- Take part in a wild picnic lunch buffet as part of a river safari outing.

- Enjoy the thrill of alligator spotting by moonlight in the jungle backwaters aboard a canoe.

- Visit a local winery to share a glass of Pettit Verdot.

Eastern Seaboard — Boston to Nassau
SEABOURN CRUISES

Colonial Harvest on the Horizon

THE BIG PICTURE

Celebrate the red, white, blue, and you on this patriotic tour of the eastern United States. Travel from Boston to Nassau with blue-blooded stops from Newport to Florida. Play George and Martha in Williamsburg, Rhett and Scarlett in Charleston, and Major Nelson and Jeannie in Cape Canaveral. Besides, you've already mastered the roles of bride and groom.

ON-BOARD ACCOMMODATIONS

The absence of ordinary is evident at every turn aboard the **Seabourn Pride**. The menu of *Pure Pampering* amenities is Seabourn's calling card, from a tray of canapés to a warm bath sprinkled with rose petals. Whatever the request, it will be magically fulfilled. (*T. 800.929.9391, www.seabourn.com*)

TOP ROMANTIC PASTIMES

- Been feeling a bit naughty of late? Delve into Puritan history at the Jamestown settlement.

- Tour the antebellum homes of the South and be ferried to each estate by horse-drawn carriage.

- Have your multi-course meal served by candlelight in your stateroom.

- Roll up your pants legs and do a little clam digging like a true New Englander.

The Mexican Riviera —
Los Angeles to Cabo San Lucas
CARNIVAL CRUISES

Affordable Elegance for Less Dinero

THE BIG PICTURE

The Pacific Ocean creates a passionate backdrop for young lovers. You'll travel to Puerto Vallarta, Mazatlán, and Cabo San Lucas, seaside destinations known for their lively villages and regional cuisine. Bargains are easy to come by ashore, something that will certainly please shopaholic newlyweds.

ON-BOARD ACCOMMODATIONS

Be lulled to sleep on the open seas. Sip salt-rimmed margaritas by moonlight. Or lounge on a deck chair and watch the world float by. If on the other hand you want to party 'til dawn, that's okay, too. Beat the odds at the Vegas-style casino or hit the nightclub for a little workout on the dance floor. Your cruise, be it mellow or manic, is what you make it. *(T. 888. CARNIVAL, www.carnival.com)*

TOP ROMANTIC PASTIMES

- Take a campy keepsake photo with the two of you wearing sombreros.

- Taste the salt air as you ride horseback along the beach.

- Go whale watching and see who spots a migrating mammal first.

- Take swimming lessons from the sea's experts— dolphins!

Celebrity

*There is only one happiness in life,
to love and be loved.*

GEORGE SAND

The Steamy Southwest

THE BIG PICTURE

Celebrities, like Goldie Hawn, often make the trek from Tinseltown to Taos to admire the art and the never-ending beauty of sagebrush and stellar sunsets. Embrace on a mesa to watch the kaleidoscopic colors at sunrise or sail over the plains in a hot air balloon. Either way, you'll both give Taos two thumbs up.

SPECIAL PLACES TO STAY

Eco-friendly and extravagant, **El Monte Sagrado** *(T. 800.828.8267, www.elmontesagrado.com)* creates a sublime setting in the Southwest. Request the ***Romance*** package featuring luxury accommodations, romantic meals, and Kama Sutra amenities, just to name a few special treats. Steps from the plaza is the historic **Taos Inn** *(T. 888.518.8267, www.taosinn.com)*. Slumber inside the inn's Helen's House, offering a handful of plush rooms with old-world charm.

TOP ROMANTIC PASTIMES

- Browse for Taos-made wares in the charming historic district.
- Mingle with the locals at a rowdy afternoon rodeo.
- Get a rush watching the Rio Grande from the nation's second highest expansion bridge.

Picture Perfect and Ultra Private

THE BIG PICTURE

The snug but glamorous town of Portofino looks like a painting at first glance, enticing you to become part of its artistry. Colorful aged buildings cluster close to the sea, stylish yachts bob in the harbor, and well-heeled couples, like yourselves, sip steamy espresso while enjoying spectacular water views.

SPECIAL PLACES TO STAY

Nestled in between the mountain and the fishermen's houses is the gracious 18-room **Hotel San Giorgio**

(T. 39.01.85.26991, www.portofinohsg.it). Each room offers stylish surroundings complete with warm yellow shades and hardwood floors. Slip away to the hidden rear garden to enjoy your morning meal. **Hotel Splendido** *(T. 39.018.526.7801, www.hotelsplendido.com)*, which counts Elizabeth Taylor among its many guests, is a former 16th-century monastery blessed with perpetual sunshine due to its east-west location. The harbor view rooms are post-card perfect, and the selection of restaurants provides an idyllic backdrop for a romantic meal.

TOP ROMANTIC PASTIMES

- Stroll the piazzetta by moonlight.
- Hike to the historic lighthouse to watch the sunrise.
- Take a sunset cruise on the harbor.
- Nibble on salty focaccia on a bench overlooking the water.

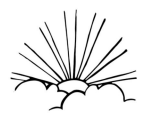

Monte Carlo

CÔTE D'AZUR, MONACO

Let the Chips Fall Where They May

THE BIG PICTURE

Overlooking the shores of the Mediterranean, Monte Carlo has always been a place to see and be seen. You'll want to sneak kisses here, there, and everywhere as you explore vaulted passageways and twisting lanes. Hit the famed casino or explore the palace where Prince Rainier and Princess Grace carried on their storybook romance.

SPECIAL PLACES TO STAY

Jutting out over the sea is the sleek **Fairmont Monte Carlo** *(T. 377.93.50.65.00, www.fairmont.com)*. With sweeping views and luxe rooms, nothing is left to chance. Book the ***Him & Her*** package, which includes deluxe sea view accommodations and a stash of casino chips. The classically elegant 1889 **Hotel Metropole, Monte-Carlo** *(T.377.93.15.15.15, www.metropole.com)* is one of the most opulent hotels. This historic property offers a spa, heated outdoor pool, and piano bar.

TOP ROMANTIC PASTIMES

- Kiss at the altar where Prince Rainier and Grace Kelly exchanged vows.
- Enjoy the million-dollar views from the hill near the palace.
- Dress to the nines, and let it ride at the world-famous Grand Casino.
- Take a romantic stroll through the beautiful Jardin Exotique.

South Beach

MIAMI, FLORIDA

Some Like It Hot

THE BIG PICTURE

If you have a penchant for spicy food and even spicier music, then pack your bags for Miami's South Beach. Celebrity regulars include Madonna and Cameron Diaz, but it's the concentration of Art Deco treasures and stylish restaurants that make this fiery enclave a star attraction. Spend your days on a beach blanket for two and your nights between 500-thread count sheets at a swank hotel.

SPECIAL PLACES TO STAY

There's a vibe taking place at **The Chesterfield Hotel** *(T. 305.531.5831, www.thechesterfieldhotel.com)*, an Art Deco treasure that now possesses a Zimbabwe-meets-baroque kind of feel. Combining 1930s glamour with sleek interiors, rooms are a steamy mix of mirrors and mahogany. Drift ashore to **The Tides Hotel** *(T. 800.439.4095, www.thetideshotel.com)*, a stylish streamlined sanctuary with a mix of ocean view accommodations, exceptional cuisine, and a pool perfect for people watching.

TOP ROMANTIC PASTIMES

- Stroll along the blush-colored sidewalks at night.
- Head to Little Havana to feast on tapas and paella.
- Surprise him by wearing a new, skimpy bikini purchased at a local boutique.
- Dance until dawn at one of the many ultra-hip velvet-roped night clubs.

Laguna Beach
ORANGE COUNTY, CALIFORNIA

Home Is Where the Art Is

THE BIG PICTURE

Laguna Beach is a haven for artists who are partial to propping easels on hillsides in hopes of capturing its beauty. But, there's nothing like the real thing. Be carried over the threshold of some charming beachfront resort, stroll the strand on a foggy morning, and sip lattes at a local coffeehouse. Time spent in Laguna Beach is time well spent.

SPECIAL PLACES TO STAY

High atop an ocean bluff and boasting impeccable service and surroundings is the exclusive **Montage Laguna Beach** *(T. 866.271.6953, www.montageresort. com)*. Book the ***Art of Romance*** package featuring an oceanfront suite plus breakfast in bed, a rose petal bath, and other amenities. Closer to the village is the **Surf & Sand Resort** *(T. 888.869.7569, www.surfand*

sandresort.com), a contemporary seaside retreat where rooms offer stunning views of the Pacific.

TOP ROMANTIC PASTIMES

- Spend the day on gallery row collecting original art.
- Commission a local artist to paint your honeymoon portrait.
- Poke around the tide pools to observe sea urchins and other underwater creatures.
- Take an outdoor painting class and create your own keepsake.

Lake Como

NORTHERN ITALY

Luxuriating Lakeside

THE BIG PICTURE

Welcome to the neighborhood. At least that's what was on the minds of the female residents of Lake Como when former "Sexiest Man Alive" George Clooney purchased his villa here. Combining

Mediterranean foliage and snowy mountain peaks, centuries-old architectural masterpieces and the simple majesty of nature, Lake Como's stunning contrasts will make your honeymoon unforgettable.

SPECIAL PLACES TO STAY

Housed in a regal 19th-century building and overlooking the mirrored waters of Lake Como is **Albergo Terminus** *(T. 031.329.111, www.hotel terminus-como.it)*. Rooms are classically appointed, the gardens magnificent, and the location enviable. The 16th-century **Villa d'Este** *(T. 39.031.3481, www.villadeste.it)* is an unbelievable hideaway that conjures up romantic possibilities at every turn. Each room is decadently different, and the lakeside location is what has lured couples here for centuries.

TOP ROMANTIC PASTIMES

- Take a romantic funicular railway ride up, up, and away to the village of Brunate.

- Uncork a bottle of bubbly while sailing the lake on a boat built for two.

- Slip between some sexy silk sheets and enjoy breakfast in bed.

Martha's Vineyard
EDGARTOWN, MASSACHUSETTS

A Safe Harbor for Honeymooners

THE BIG PICTURE

Celebrities such as David Letterman and Carly Simon are no strangers to Martha's Vineyard. It's not the name-dropping that makes this an A-list destination, though, but rather the simple pleasures. Roll out of bed together, hunt for shells on the beach, and spend a lazy day angling from a tiny wooden boat. Who cares if you return empty handed? You've already reeled in your big fish!

SPECIAL PLACES TO STAY

Far removed from the souvenir kitsch is the charming hamlet of Edgartown. Here you'll find the turreted **Harbor View Hotel** *(T. 800.225.6005, www. harbor-view.com),* offering the quintessential vineyard escape with lighthouse views and a collection of delightful rooms. The nearby 14-room **Victorian Inn**

(T. 508.627.4784, www.thevic.com), built for a 19th-century whaling captain, is now an elegant bed and breakfast. Each stay includes a gourmet breakfast and afternoon tea.

TOP ROMANTIC PASTIMES

- Head to the beach for a traditional New England clambake.

- Rent a two-seat convertible and cruise the entire island in style.

- Take a twirl on the nation's oldest carousel.

- Explore one of the historic lighthouses that dot the island.

East Hampton

LONG ISLAND, NEW YORK

Hobnobbing in the Hamptons

THE BIG PICTURE

Touted as a playground for the rich and famous, East Hampton has welcomed its share of celebrities, from Jacqueline Kennedy to Jerry Seinfeld. You, too, can enjoy the star treatment. Wander along the beaches at dusk, duck inside a café for a romantic meal, and avail yourself of some of the cultural treasures of the Hamptons, such as the paint-splattered studio where artist Jackson Pollock created his most admired work.

SPECIAL PLACES TO STAY

With just a handful of rooms and a picturesque location, the 1790 **Mill House Inn** (*T. 631.324.9766, www. millhouseinn.com*) offers exquisite chambers with varying influences plus a full breakfast. **East Hampton Point** (*T. 631.324.9191, www.easthamptonpoint.com*) features a collection of cottages and suites, many with fabulous views and private decks.

TOP ROMANTIC PASTIMES

- Make sand angels on Main Beach.

- Do a little wine sampling—Hamptons style—at a handful of tasting barns.

- Snag a two-person kayak and explore the harbor's breathtaking beauty.

- Visit the village bookstore and start a two-person book club.

- Feast on a sunset picnic at the town pond.

Maui
HAWAIIAN ISLANDS

Eat, Drink, and See Maui

THE BIG PICTURE

Everything about Maui is magical, from its pristine coastline to its lush landscape. Even the famous, such as Cindy Crawford and Heather Locklear, are mesmerized by its mystique. Lose count of the waterfalls, scan the seas for humpback whales, or take a hand-holding hike to the Haleakala Crater. Come evening, work a little magic of your own by pulling a disappearing act behind the door of your hotel suite.

SPECIAL PLACES TO STAY

The all-suite **Fairmont Kea Lani Maui** *(T. 808. 875.4100, www.fairmont.com)* offers an extravagant escape with its *Honi Honi Romance* package, complete with romantic meals, a tandem massage, and more. Or retreat to the secluded **Hotel Hana-Maui** *(T. 808.248.8211, www.hotelhanamaui.com)* at the end of the Hana Highway. A sea ranch cottage offers island heritage, natural beauty, and a private retreat where all you'll hear is the rustle of palm trees.

TOP ROMANTIC PASTIMES

- Watch the sunrise atop the Haleakala Crater.
- Take a scenic drive along Hana Highway.
- Climb aboard a historic train for a time travel journey.
- Lounge beneath Hawaii's largest banyan tree.
- Spell your names out in shells along the beach.

Cannes
FRENCH RIVIERA

Always Ready for Its Close-Up

THE BIG PICTURE

Cannes is transformed into a never-ending ribbon of red carpet during the annual film festival. Ah, but when it comes to honeymoons, it's the two of you who are creating headlines. Select stems from the colorful flower market, share a steaming bowl of café latte at an espresso bar, or graze on freshly picked cherries from the farmers' market.

SPECIAL PLACES TO STAY

Located in a quiet neighborhood, **Renoir** *(T. 04.92. 99.62.62, www.hotel-renoir-cannes.com)* evokes the feel of a weekend *maison*. The hotel features just a handful of rooms, many with kitchenettes, so you can pretend you've acquired your very own *pied-à-terre*. Overlooking the yacht harbor is the **Hotel Splendid** *(T. 04.97.06.22.22, www.splendid-hotel-cannes.fr)*, which lives up to its name. The selection of rooms offers an abundance of thoughtful touches.

TOP ROMANTIC PASTIMES

- Drive along the Côte d'Azur from the French Riviera to the Italian border.

- Flirt with one-armed bandits at Casino Croisette.

- Make your honeymoon a Hollywood production by arriving in time for the film festival.

- Give yourselves a housewarming gift from the antiques market in nearby Nice.

Park City
UTAH

Lights, Camera, and Plenty of Action

THE BIG PICTURE

Robert Redford is credited with putting this alpine town on the map when he launched the Sundance Film Festival, which creates celebrity gridlock on both the sidewalks and slopes. But you'll want to limit your stargazing to those twinkling in the crisp Utah sky. Go rock climbing, try skiing, or just snuggle up together in front of a roaring fire. Your time together here is virtually unscripted.

SPECIAL PLACES TO STAY

Lessons in love are at play inside **Washington School Inn** *(T. 800.824.1672, www.washingtonschoolinn.com)*, a former 1889 limestone schoolhouse. Fifteen charming rooms boast oversized classroom windows and hidden dormers. The newly-built, all-suite **Hotel Park City** *(T. 435.200.2000, www.hotelparkcity.com)* is reminiscent of a grand lodge. It's full-service and fabulous, with fine dining and spa services.

TOP ROMANTIC PASTIMES

- Tear up the mountain together on a snowmobile outing.

- Jump on a heaping pile of leaves while enjoying the fall foliage.

- Cuddle close on a full moon lift ride to the top of the mountain.

- Surprise each other with a trinket you crafted at a silversmithing class.

Aspen

COLORADO

Romance in the Rockies

THE BIG PICTURE

Aspen's first snowfall brings the celebrities out in full force—the Tom Cruises, Kevin Costners and members of the Kennedy clan. Still, you're more interested in sharing the spotlight with your significant other. Take part in the social whirlwind of gallery openings and chatty wine bars. Or better yet, hit the slopes in the morning and sequester yourselves behind closed doors at night.

SPECIAL PLACES TO STAY

The Little Nell *(T. 970.920.4600, www.thelittle nell.com)* is Aspen's only ski-in/ski-out resort. Well-appointed rooms are warmed by fireplaces, and the bar is frequented by famous faces. **The Sky Hotel** *(T. 800.882.2582, www.theskyhotel.com)* combines high style with playfulness. Its slopeside location and whimsical ways are geared to those with a curiosity for the cutting edge. Rooms are boldly appointed and feature iPod docking stations and other gadgets.

TOP ROMANTIC PASTIMES

- Shop for local pottery at the weekly farmers' market.
- Purify your bodies at the nearby vapor caves.
- Park yourselves on a bench near the fountain and enjoy the talents of local musicians.
- Canoodle to chamber music at the summer Aspen Music Festival.

Jackson Hole
WYOMING

Life Can Be Tantalizing
beneath the Grand Tetons

THE BIG PICTURE

Jackson Hole is no stranger to Hollywood. Not only has it served as the backdrop for several movies, including the 1950s tearjerker *Shane*, it is also popular with celebrities like Harrison Ford. Star power aside, Jackson Hole is full of natural beauty coupled with just a tinge of tinsel. Sail down the slopes on a snow tube or pick wildflowers at first bloom. Like any good director, only you can call the shots.

SPECIAL PLACES TO STAY

Enjoy ski-in/ski-out access at the luxurious **Four Seasons Resort** *(T. 307.732.5000, www.four seasons.com)*. Book the spectacular **Honeymoon Adventure** with luxurious accommodations, champagne, strawberries, meals, massages, and seasonal outdoor activities. Nearby is the remarkable

Teton Mountain Lodge *(T. 800.801.6615, www.teton lodge.com)*, with its collection of rustically romantic rooms promoting a "home away from home" ambiance with living areas, kitchens, and bedrooms.

TOP ROMANTIC PASTIMES

- See how many bison you can spot from a distance.
- Do a little dog-sledding out on the range.
- Take a ride down the rapids of the winding Snake River.
- Ride off into the sunset on horseback.

Classic

Love is the greatest refreshment in life.

PABLO PICASSO

Palm Springs

CALIFORNIA

Mid-century Chic

THE BIG PICTURE

Palm Springs. The name alone is enough to ignite your hunger for romance. Plan on doing nothing more than lounging poolside and sharing salt-rimmed margaritas the size of Mexico. You might also want to do a little foreplay on the golf course and, of course, there's always time for a tandem mud bath at some posh spa.

SPECIAL PLACES TO STAY

The Spanish-style **La Quinta Resort & Club** *(T. 800.598.3828, www.laquintaresort.com)* is a historic and spacious find. There are several free-

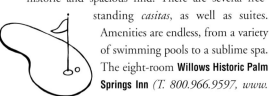

standing *casitas*, as well as suites. Amenities are endless, from a variety of swimming pools to a sublime spa. The eight-room **Willows Historic Palm Springs Inn** *(T. 800.966.9597, www.*

thewillowspalmsprings.com) is extraordinarily romantic, and guests enjoy complimentary breakfast and evening wine.

TOP ROMANTIC PASTIMES

- Soar to the top of Mt. San Jacinto aboard the Palm Springs Aerial Tramway.

- Enjoy a side-by-side outdoor mud bath at the famed **Two Bunch Palms** resort.

- Saddle up for a horseback ride through the desert.

Las Vegas

NEVADA

A Sure Bet for Round-the-clock Romance

THE BIG PICTURE

Travel the world together in just a few blocks with a trip to Paris, New York, or Venice. Sin City has everything you could possibly want or need 24/7. Hedge your bets at the gaming tables by night, then sleep the day away in a private poolside cabana. The Vegas skyline may look different from when Frank and Sammy ruled the town, but the attitude hasn't changed.

SPECIAL PLACES TO STAY

If you're longing for a little elegance along the Las Vegas Strip, **Bellagio** *(T. 702.693.7111, www. bellagio.com)* is a safe bet. In a town known for kitsch, this resort offers few gimmicks. Rooms are elegant and the restaurants refined. Synchronized fountains erupt, Fantasia-style, in a massive man-made lake fronting Bellagio. If you've always dreamt of a Parisian honeymoon, you'll both be in your element at **Paris Las Vegas** *(T. 877.603.4386, www. harrahs.com)*. From the replicated Arc de Triomphe to the sound of accordion music wafting down indoor cobblestone streets, it's a *très bon* experience. When you're in the mood for a change, head to more faux Las Vegas locales, such as Luxor, Rio, or Monte Carlo.

TOP ROMANTIC PASTIMES

- Enjoy a midnight dinner at the top of the Eiffel Tower at Paris Las Vegas.

- Make a day of it with a helicopter ride over the Grand Canyon.

- Embark on a sunset champagne hot air balloon flight above the desert terrain.

- Enjoy Cirque du Soleil's *Zumanity*, an erotic show that celebrates love.

- Hold on tight—to each other—at the top of the Stratosphere Tower, where you can ride *The Big Shot* thrill ride 1,081 feet above the Vegas Strip.

Pocono Mountains

PENNSYLVANIA

All You Need Is Love

THE BIG PICTURE

For decades brides and grooms have headed for the Pennsylvania hills to celebrate their newly-married status. The area is famous for its scenic beauty—and even more renowned for its indoor activities. Honeymooners are lured up the mountain with promises of heart-shaped beds and bathtubs fashioned after champagne glasses.

You, too, will enjoy the naughty nuances of this honeymoon haven. With room service available morning, noon, and night, there's no need to ever venture beyond your guest room door.

SPECIAL PLACES TO STAY

Opt for one of the many couples-only lodges, such as **Cove Haven Resort** *(T. 877.822.3333, www. caesarspoconoresorts.com)* or **Paradise Stream Resort** *(T. 877.822.3333, www.caesarspoconoresorts.com)*. Both offer all-inclusive stays, sensuous accommodations, including in suite indoor pools, and honeymoon concierges to make sure every romantic detail is handled.

TOP ROMANTIC PASTIMES

- Take a thrilling white water rafting ride through the scenic wooded landscape.

- Saddle up for a long, leisurely horseback ride.

- Take a bubble bath *à deux* in your champagne glass tub.

- Be a contestant in the Newlywed/Not-So Newlywed game at the Cove Haven Resort.

- Take a long lakeside walk together at sunrise.

Niagara Falls

CANADA

Take a Wet and Wild Plunge

THE BIG PICTURE

Straddling the American-Canadian border are the spectacular Niagara Falls. Honeymooners like yourselves have been making the pilgrimage to this wet and wild wonderland for years. In New York State you can view the American and Bridal Veil falls, but a more spectacular cascade of water, Horseshoe Falls, is found on the other side of the border. Wake up in maple leaf country, where you can view this gushing spectacle from the comfort of your oversized bed.

SPECIAL PLACES TO STAY

For nearly 80 years, the **Brock Plaza Hotel** *(T. 800.236.7135, www.niagarafallshotels.com/brock)* has welcomed both Hollywood and reigning royalty. After undergoing a major renovation, the vintage hotel still offers classic 1920s appointments. Best of all, nearly every room features million-dollar views.

Opt for the *Honeymoon* package at the thoroughly modern **Sheraton Fallsview Hotel** *(T. 800.618.9059, www.fallsview.com)*. Included are accommodations with views of the falls, welcome wine and cheese, a lavish breakfast buffet, and late checkout.

TOP ROMANTIC PASTIMES

- Take a romantic horse-drawn carriage ride along the falls.

- Don't miss the Winter Festival of Lights, featuring 34,000 tree-draped lights near the Rainbow Bridge.

- Snuggle close on a misted summer evening and enjoy the spectacular display of weekend fireworks.

- Glide together above the Niagara River in a vintage cable car-like gondola.

Walt Disney World
FLORIDA

The Land of Make-believe

THE BIG PICTURE

If you didn't know each other during childhood, here's your chance to act like kids again—together. Visit Disney's four theme parks, and enjoy such simple pleasures as giant snow cones, chocolate-dipped ice cream bars, and parading about in Mickey Mouse hats. Allow yourselves to be uninhibited and, dare we say, goofy?

SPECIAL PLACES TO STAY

Consider booking a Disney honeymoon, which offfers an all-inclusive package of accommodations, dining, recreation, and theme park tours. Disney has many hotels, but the intimate Victorian-style **Boardwalk Inn and Villas** *(T. 407.939.5100, www. disneyworld.com)* captures the feel of an old-fashioned New England coastal compound. Request a room overlooking Crescent Lake for some added romance. The luxurious **Buena Vista Palace Hotel & Spa** *(T. 866.397.6516, www.buenavistapalace.com)* is located in Downtown Disney, and features rooms with patios or balconies. Visit the lounge on the 27th floor, where you can watch the sunset and enjoy a cocktail.

TOP ROMANTIC PASTIMES

- Have your silhouettes drawn at the artist shop along the Magic Kingdom's Main Street.

- Pass time while standing on line at the Pirates of the Caribbean by singing the words to "A Pirate's Life for Me."

- Feed each other exotic foods at Epcot's international pavilions.

- Cling to each other on the Primeval Whirl in Animal Kingdom.

- Watch the classic love tale, Beauty and the Beast— Live on Stage, in Disney's Hollywood Studios.

Venice
ITALY

Saints, Squares, and Serenades—That's Amore!

THE BIG PICTURE

Venice is one of those places that just seem destined for lovers. You're bound to find yourselves strolling arm-and-arm along the canals, noshing on *cicchetti* atop some ancient bridge, or slipping into a wine bar for a glass of aged Chianti. Wander the narrow passageways, which lead to ancient piazzas, renowned galleries, and welcome surprises.

SPECIAL PLACES TO STAY

With only 14 rooms overlooking a narrow waterway, **Ca Maria Adele** (*T. 39.041.520.3078, www.camaria adele.it*) offers dramatic digs. Honeymooners can book a special getaway that includes a full breakfast, welcome drink, a visit to a Murano glass factory, and gondola tour with Prosecco wine. Behind the gold-rimmed doors of the 16th-century **Hotel Gritti Palace**

(*T. 39.041.794.611, www.starwoodhotels.com*), the former residence of the Doge of Venice, are some of the most elegant rooms, both private and public, and amazing views of the Grand Canal. Former guests include the likes of the Queen of England and Winston Churchill—oh, if only the walls could talk!

TOP ROMANTIC PASTIMES

- Enjoy a serenade along the Grand Canal by a seasoned gondolier.
- Stroll along the Lido holding hands.
- Enjoy a romantic lunch of red wine, dry salami, and plump olives in Piazza San Marco.
- Pucker up under the Bridge of Sighs, then head to a nearby market to shop for treasures.

Charleston

SOUTH CAROLINA

A Sampling of Southern Comfort

THE BIG PICTURE

Follow in the footsteps of Scarlett O'Hara and Rhett Butler, who spent their fictional honeymoon in this charming antebellum city. So civilized and yet so sexy, this southern port town provides a perfect balance between traditional and trendy. One minute you're wandering through a Civil War-era plantation, and the next you're noshing on nouvelle cuisine at some hip eatery. Oh, fiddle-dee-dee.

SPECIAL PLACES TO STAY

The 64-room **Planter's Inn** *(T. 843.722.2345, www.plantersinn.com)*, built in the mid 1800s, is where historic elegance and modern luxury live in complete harmony. Slumber in rooms graced with high ceilings, antiques, and roomy four-poster, canopied beds. Enjoy the inn's ***Elegant Interlude*** escape featuring fresh-cut flowers, a bottle of

 champagne, a pair of mono-grammed champagne flutes and robes to match, daily breakfast, and cognac and chocolate truffles at turndown. As if plucked from the pages of a history book, the Gilded Age **Wentworth Mansion** *(T. 888.466.1886, www.wentworthmansion.com)* is one of Charleston's finest homes. Corners aren't cut; complimentary treats include stocked in-room refrigerators, a plentiful breakfast, and afternoon spirits.

TOP ROMANTIC PASTIMES

- Let a horse-drawn carriage ferry you on a self-guided tour of the city's many antebellum homes.
- Enjoy a simple evening stroll, inhaling the honeysuckle and jasmine that permeate the air.
- Take in the arts at the annual spring Spoleto Festival USA.
- Explore the tidal slough and Cooper River in a two-person kayak.

Acapulco

MEXICO

Cliff Dives, Discos, and Daily Siestas

THE BIG PICTURE

For years lovers have flocked south of the border for a spicy start to the happily ever after. You'll find Acapulco can be as lively or as laid back as you wish. The beaches are beautiful, the weather enviable, and the nightlife is hot. The two of you can dance until dawn at a hip nightclub or better yet, make your own music in the privacy of your plush hacienda.

SPECIAL PLACES TO STAY

Feel pampered and pink at the blush-colored **Las Brisas** *(T. 800.223.6800, www.brisas.com.mx)*, a legendary hilltop resort where free-standing rooms come with their own swimming pools, and guests are chauffeured about in classic pink Jeeps. If you're looking for that "wow" factor, you'll find it at the former J. Paul Getty estate turned **Fairmont Pierre**

Marques *(T. 800.441.1414, www.fairmont.com)*. This kiss-worthy resort is near the water's edge and offers full-service satisfaction.

TOP ROMANTIC PASTIMES

- Take a romantic cruise around Acapulco Bay while listening to live music.
- Enjoy an evening cliff-diving show at La Quebrada, home to 100-foot cliffs.
- Explore the *zócalo*, the city's bustling town center.
- Enjoy a boat tour in the picturesque Coyuca Lagoon.

Waikiki Beach

HAWAII

Surf, Sand, and Sun-kissed Skies

THE BIG PICTURE

Welcome to paradise, where days are spent barefoot on platinum sands, frolicking in bluer-than-blue waters, and feeding each other juicy chunks of fresh pineapple. Come evening a fleet of tiki torches is all aglow up and down the shoreline as you partake in a luau, learning the traditions and rituals of the Hawaiian culture under a thatch of swaying palms.

SPECIAL PLACES TO STAY

From multiple pools to black-footed penguins, **Hilton Hawaiian Village** *(T. 808.949. 4321,www.hiltonhawaiianvillage.com)* has it all. Request a room in the allur-ing **Ali'i Tower**, a resort within a resort with its own private pool and thrice-daily maid service. Or say aloha to the historic and legendary **Royal Hawaiian Hotel** *(T. 866.716.8109,*

www.royal-hawaiian.com), better known as "The Pink Palace of the Pacific." Request an original oceanfront room along with the **Romance** package featuring welcome wine and cheese plus daily breakfast served in your room.

TOP ROMANTIC PASTIMES

- Learn to hula like a Hawaiian native.
- Go swimming with the dolphins.
- Hike to a hidden waterfall.
- Go kayaking in search of sea turtles.
- Hang ten with his and her surfing lessons.

Atlantic City
NEW JERSEY

Under the Boardwalk at the Jersey Shore

THE BIG PICTURE

Atlantic City, the former home of the Miss America Pageant, is a lot like Vegas, only this gambling haven has something Sin City doesn't—a beach. Wander the boardwalk in search of lady luck. Enjoy the afternoon at the beach or share a mound of cotton candy from a seaside kiosk. Feeling lucky? Then skip the urge to tug at one-arm bandits and head to the privacy of your ocean view room instead.

SPECIAL PLACES TO STAY

The best rooms in Atlantic City are at the plush **Borgata Hotel Casino & Spa** *(T. 609.317-1000, www.theborgata.com)*, where expansive windows, stylish décor, and tandem showers create a haven for honeymooners. Situated on the boardwalk is **Bally's** *(T. 609.340.2000, www.ballysac.com)*, with a myriad of traditional and contemporary rooms. Check out the sublime spa and its decadent choice of treatments.

TOP ROMANTIC PASTIMES

- Toast your good fortune at one of the beach bars.
- Play footsy while enjoying a couples massage.
- Build your dream house out of sand on the beach.
- Pretend you're competing for Miss America, and stage a private swimsuit competition for your honey.

Savannah

GEORGIA

Historic, Haunted, with Shades of "Haint Blue"

THE BIG PICTURE

Savannah is a genteel river town with an eccentric edge. Steeped in superstition, yet with all the charm of a southern belle, it affords enchantment at every turn. Explore the historic district and its assembly of town squares punctuated with fountains and feathered Spanish moss. Entrances are often coated in "haint blue" to ward off restless apparitions. However, the only spirits you're likely to encounter are the refreshing mint juleps.

SPECIAL PLACES TO STAY

Located in the historic district is **The Gastonian** (*T. 912.232.2869, www.gastonian.com*), a 17-room

bed and breakfast created from a pair of 1868 mansions. Your stay includes a gourmet breakfast, afternoon wine and tea, and evening cordials with dessert. The

1847 **Eliza Thompson House** *(T. 800.348.9378, www.elizathompsonhouse.com)* is located on one of Savannah's most gracious streets, with rooms divided among the main manor and carriage house.

TOP ROMANTIC PASTIMES

- Stroll arm-in-arm beneath canopies of live oaks along Melon Bluff.

- Visit Bonaventure Cemetery, where aged headstones tell of Savannah's past.

- Sip grog with your matey at an 18th-century tavern once frequented by pirates.

- Take a heady walk along St. Julian Street, where colonists burned oyster shells to make cement.

Lake Tahoe

CALIFORNIA/NEVADA

One Lake, Two States, Endless Activities

THE BIG PICTURE

If the two of you are split on how to spend your honeymoon, Lake Tahoe can be a neutralizing force. The great outdoors beckons on the California side: lazy canoe rides, hikes to secluded peaks, and downhill skiing in near perfect powder. Cross the state line to Nevada for glittering casinos and endless indoor entertainment. Both halves complete the whole Tahoe experience.

SPECIAL PLACES TO STAY

Clustered together near the lake, **Rustic Cottage Resorts** (*T. 888.778.7842, www.rusticcottages.com*) offers simple and charming bungalows. Snuggle tight in a vintage bed, cuddle in front of the fire, or watch the sunset from your porch. From homey to heavenly, the **Black Bear Inn** (*T. 877.232.7466, www.tahoeblack bear.com*) features tasteful, old Tahoe-style guest rooms and freestanding cottages. It's centrally located and unabashedly luxurious, and you'll awake each morning to a hearty breakfast.

TOP ROMANTIC PASTIMES

- Feeling hot? Find a secluded cove and go skinny dipping.
- Race each other down the slopes; winner receives a massage from the loser.
- Ride the cable car to High Camp for sunset cocktails with panoramic views.

Island & Beachfront

Life is a journey, and love is what makes that journey worthwhile.

AUTHOR UNKNOWN

When It Comes to Romance,
Greece Is the Word

THE BIG PICTURE

Looking like an airbrushed painting of alabaster structures and cobalt blue accents is the splendid island of Mykonos. Spend your days lounging on the beach (a clothing-optional one, perhaps?) and your nights at some sultry *taverna*. Walk the village, sneak a kiss in some narrow passageway, and nibble on Greek specialties at a charming café while the world fades away.

SPECIAL PLACES TO STAY

Villa Konstantin *(T. 30.22890.26204, www.villa konstantin-mykonos.gr)* is a complex of simple, traditional flats with town and ocean views. Retreat to your air-conditioned lovers studio with its own kitchen and terrace. Intimately intriguing, the 40-chamber **Kivotos Clubhotel Deluxe** *(T.30.22890.25795,* *www.kivotosclubhotel.gr)* conceals a collection of alluring rooms with beds sheathed in gauze and romantic Juliet-style balconies.

TOP ROMANTIC PASTIMES

- Get a romantic rush with a parasail above the Aegean Sea.
- Enjoy a twilight toast at a sidewalk café in Little Venice.
- Snap a honeymoon photo in front of the charming Mykonos windmills.

Kauai

HAWAIIAN ISLANDS

Welcome to the Garden of Eden

THE BIG PICTURE

Get ready for romps in the surf and long caresses beneath cascading waterfalls. Kauai is like forbidden fruit, tempting twosomes with its lush landscapes and platinum sands. Leave the busy world behind as you relax in the warm waters or indulge each other at a five-star retreat. This, by the way, sounds like the idyllic honeymoon.

SPECIAL PLACES TO STAY

Overlooking Hanalei Bay is the stunning **Princeville Resort** *(T. 808.826. 9644, www.princevillehotelhawaii.com)*, where you'll slumber in dreamy rooms, swim in the seaside infinity pool, and dine on mouthwatering cuisine. You'll find little reason to venture from the beachfront **Grand Hyatt Kauai Resort & Spa** *(T. 808. 742.1234, www.kauai.hyatt.com)* in Koloa. The stylish rooms, savory restaurants, and abundance of amenities will make you stay put.

TOP ROMANTIC PASTIMES

- Arrange for a private torch-lit dinner along Hanalei Bay.

- Take a kayak journey along the Wailua River.

- Hike to Fern Grotto and sway à la Tarzan and Jane on a rope swing.

- Venture to one of the island's many waterfalls for an *au naturel* shower.

Coronado Island

SAN DIEGO, CALIFORNIA

The Land of Aahs

THE BIG PICTURE

Contrary to belief, Coronado Island is actually a peninsula. It's famous for one thing and one thing only—the historic Hotel Del Coronado. Explore the turreted palace for signs of restless spirits—the hotel is rumored to be haunted. Or take a quick ferry ride across the harbor to downtown San Diego. Better yet, stay put in paradise, and keep the world at bay.

SPECIAL PLACES TO STAY

For locals, honeymooning at **Hotel del Coronado** (*T. 619.435.6611, www.hoteldel.com*) is a rite of passage. Its gingerbread façade is believed to have been the inspiration for the Emerald City in *The Wizard of Oz*. Your lifelong romance begins here, beneath the roof of this lovely legend. Slumber in an oversized Victorian room or request a plush, new cottage at the stylish Beach Village. This waterfront wonderland has it all—restaurants, shops, lounges, and pools.

TOP ROMANTIC PASTIMES

- Enjoy an outdoor summer concert with the locals.

- Take a romantic gondola ride around the cays.

- Set sail for a sunset dinner cruise.

- Tour the island on a charming two-seater surrey cycle.

Isle of Capri
SOUTHERN ITALY

Feeling Blue off the Amalfi Coast

THE BIG PICTURE

Flee the mainland—even if it's only a three-mile jaunt—to lovely Capri, known as "the blue island." Dramatic and decidedly romantic, the island will

mesmerize you with its charismatic setting. Dance cheek-to-cheek among flower-filled courtyards, skip along the winding streets, and enjoy the intoxicating aroma of freshly plucked lemons. Go ahead, and pucker up!

SPECIAL PLACES TO STAY

Sequester yourselves inside **J.K. Place Capri** *(T. 39.081.838.4001, www.jkcapri.com)*, a 22-room retreat with stunning sea views. Soak in an oversized tub, slip on your robes, and sip champagne  on your bougainvillea-draped terrace. Boasting a commanding cliffside locale is **Caesar Augustus** *(T. 39.081. 837.3395, www.caesar-augustus.com)*, the former home of a Russian prince. This stately villa offers honeymooners a special treat of flowers and champagne upon arrival, candlelight dinner, private island boat tour, and massage for two.

TOP ROMANTIC PASTIMES

- Climb inside a rowboat and explore the marvelous Blue Grotto.

- Find a remote cove for a lazy afternoon picnic and swim.

- Learn the tarantella, an ancient Italian folk dance.

- Get a his and her lesson in Capri-style cooking.

Two Tickets to Paradise

THE BIG PICTURE

If you had any concerns about paradise being lost, relax—it's been found. Welcome to the Turks & Caicos Islands, a Caribbean archipelago with eight inhabited islands, including the 1,000-acre Parrot Cay. Enjoy a bit of escapism as you dig your toes in the velvety sands for a playful game of footsy. Time has little meaning in this part of the world.

SPECIAL PLACES TO STAY

Be cosseted with not a care in the world at **Parrot Cay** *(T. 877.754.0726, www.parrotcay.como.bz)*, a private and posh island resort. Newlyweds are especially pampered with a seven-day ***Summer Honeymooning*** package. Included are a luxurious suite, daily breakfast and dinner, champagne upon arrival, a half-day spa indulgence, non-motorized water sports, and daily workout classes.

TOP ROMANTIC PASTIMES

- Comb the beaches for sand dollar souvenirs.

- Hold hands and swim with the fishes on a scuba diving expedition.

- Sail around the island by moonlight on a former rum runner.

- Arrange for a private beach barbecue complete with umbrella-topped drinks.

Unlock the Magic to These Heavenly Islands

THE BIG PICTURE

The Florida Keys have all the trappings of a tropical paradise: swaying palm trees, balmy breezes, and billowy sailboats. The legions of islands are connected by bridges and causeways, but you can disconnect at any one of them. Pretend you're Papa and Pauline Hemingway as you prowl about Key West. Try a new adventure—maybe a swim with the dolphins? Then slip inside a poolside cabana for a little alone time.

SPECIAL PLACES TO STAY

Located three miles offshore on a palm-fringed island is what some call the "wow" factor—**Little Palm Island** (*T. 800.343.8567, www.littlepalmisland.com*). Every want, need, and desire is fulfilled here, and honeymooners can take it a step further with the ***Get Lost*** package. Upon arrival you're whisked away to a private, phone-free bungalow, greeted with champagne, spoiled with breakfast, and pampered at the spa. Just 16 suites are found at **Casa Morada** (*T. 888.881.3030, www.casamorada.com*), located on the bay in Islamorada. Abodes feature both indoor and private outdoor spaces.

TOP ROMANTIC PASTIMES

- Enjoy a scenic boat ride to the Florida Everglades.
- Intertwine your bodies on an oversized hammock for two.
- Quietly wade in the water together on a fly-fishing expedition.
- Go retro with a friendly game of croquet.

Montego Bay

JAMAICA

One Love, One Heart

THE BIG PICTURE

Jamaica, especially Montego Bay, is the land of no worries. Blessed by the kindness of Mother Nature, it's a place of sun-kissed skies sheltered by the rustle of swaying palms. Check into the resort and check out the romantic possibilities—horseback rides along the beach, carefree walks at sunset, and nights under the star-filled skies.

SPECIAL PLACES TO STAY

There's nothing half-hearted about **Half Moon** *(T. 876.953.2211, www. halfmoon.com)*, an incredible, full-service resort where every desire has been anticipated. Embark on a *Romantic Rendezvous* where you'll enjoy luxurious accommodations, champagne, private dinner, spa treatments, and more. Not to be outdone is **Round Hill Hotel and Villas** *(T. 876.956.7050, www.roundhill*

jamaica.com), featuring three dozen rooms plus some 27 freestanding villas replete with personal maid, cook, and private pools.

TOP ROMANTIC PASTIMES

- Head to the waterfalls to soak together in one of the natural pools.
- Do a little crocodile hunting—if you dare—on a Black River Safari.
- Build a castle of golden sand on the beach.
- Explore the colorful coral reefs on a snorkeling expedition.

North Malé Atoll
THE MALDIVES

Low-key Luxury

THE BIG PICTURE

Strewn across the Indian Ocean like a strand of pearls are thousands of tiny islands. Take the plunge—again—only this time into one of the many placid lagoons. Find your *om* during a couples yoga class or engage in a friendly game of beach volleyball. At night, the only sounds you'll hear are the lapping waves that sweep across the shore and, perhaps, some contented sighs from within the confines of your honeymoon hideaway.

SPECIAL PLACES TO STAY

Occupying a private island is **Full Moon Maldives** *(T.960.664.2010, www.fullmoonmaldives.com),* a serene sanctuary featuring a collection of over-the-water thatched villas and beachfront cottages. Equally enticing is **Huvafen Fushi** *(T. 960.664.4222, www.huvafenfushi.com),* set within its very own lagoon. Choose from a menu of accommodations, from bungalows boasting plunge pools to villas that seem to float above water.

TOP ROMANTIC PASTIMES

- Explore the lagoons in a two-person canoe.
- Arrange for a private dinner in an underground wine cellar.
- Drift out to sea on an oversized raft.
- Charter a yacht and cruise to some uninhabited island.

Palm Trees and Piña Coladas

THE BIG PICTURE

Now that you've shed the Vera Wang gown, along with the tails or tux, fill the suitcase with swimsuits—lots of swimsuits. That's all you need on this tropical island. Make love on a deserted beach by the moonlight as wild horses fan across the shoreline in the distance. Is this real or are you dreaming? You may need to pinch each other from time to time—which can also be quite fun!

SPECIAL PLACES TO STAY

Rising from the lobby of the 16-room **Hacienda Tamarindo** *(T. 787.741.0420, www.haciendatama rindo.com)* is a striking tamarind tree, creating a visual statement from the onset. You'll slumber in a cozy room that likely overlooks the Caribbean, with incredible 180-degree views. Eco-friendly and completely crafted from concrete, **Hix Island House** *(T. 787.741.2302, www.hixislandhouse.com)* is *über* cool and minimalist by nature. Rooms are uncluttered yet comfortable with open-air showers that offer plenty of privacy.

TOP ROMANTIC PASTIMES

- Take to the dance floor to show off your salsa skills.
- Share a piña colada, Puerto Rico's signature thirst quencher.
- Nibble on *mofongo*, an island specialty of pan-fried plantains.
- Collect seashells from one of the deserted beaches.

Bonaire
DUTCH CARIBBEAN

Lazy Days and Dreamy Nights

THE BIG PICTURE

The days can be hot on Bonaire, but for newlyweds the nights may be even steamier. Stake your claim on the sandy pink beach as the turquoise waters playfully inch closer. Afternoons tend to be long and lazy and the midnight hour a bit bewitching. As for how to keep busy, well there just isn't a lot to do and isn't that really the reason for being here?

SPECIAL PLACES TO STAY

Opening onto a swath of sand is the pastel painted **Harbour Village Beach Club** *(T. 599.717.7500, www.harbourvillage.com)*, where rooms are romantically appointed. The resort's beach club is abuzz with activity, while the day spa provides a taste of tranquility. With just five guest rooms to choose from, you could likely have the run of **The Deep Blue View** *(T. 599.717.8073, www.deepblueview.com)*. This intimate bed and breakfast resort offers incredible views and personal service.

TOP ROMANTIC PASTIMES

- Take a dive below the water's surface for the most striking views.

- Skip the spa and give each other a soothing massage.

- Puff on a Cuban cigar and graze on tapas in Little Havana.

Tea Time at the Empress

THE BIG PICTURE

Stroll along the cobbled streets of Victoria beneath dangling baskets of blooming flowers. Much of downtown has been restored to its original Victorian splendor with historic homes looking as if they've been ripped from the pages of a Jane Austen novel. And, like any proper couple, you'll likely partake in the ritual of afternoon tea.

SPECIAL PLACES TO STAY

The century-old **Fairmont Empress Hotel** *(T. 250.384.8111, www.fairmont.com)* is *the* place to stay while in Victoria. The marvelous Edwardian landmark offers a handsome lot of historic rooms coupled

with impeccable service. ***The Lovers' Escape*** package provides all the amenities needed for a fabulous honeymoon, including roomy accommodations, a romantic three-course dinner for two, breakfast in bed, a decadent chocolate treat, and a "romance-to-go" kit.

TOP ROMANTIC PASTIMES

- Enjoy the summer fireworks and music at the magnificent Butchart Gardens.

- Marvel at the stunning sunset views that frame the Olympic Mountains.

- Grab a cup of coffee and watch the sun rise over the inner harbor.

- Graze on scones served with clotted cream and strawberry preserves at the Empress's elegant afternoon tea.

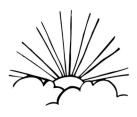

Anguilla

BRITISH WEST INDIES

Fabulously Far-flung

THE BIG PICTURE

If you love the beach, Anguilla has one for every day of the month. In this uncrowded paradise, you'll have room to bask beneath the cloudless skies or explore the island by bicycle. If only every day on the mainland could be like this.

SPECIAL PLACES TO STAY

Enjoy being coddled at the insulated **Cap Juluca** *(T. 264.497.6666, www.capjuluca.com)*, a private enclave with marvelous Moorish villas and stellar five-star dining, fronted by a stretch of platinum-sand beach. Overlooking Meads Bay is the **Malliouhana Hotel & Spa** *(T. 800.835.0796, www.malliouhana.com)* where the extraordinary is the norm. The ***Romantic Interlude*** offers lovers ocean view accommodations, wine and petit fours, daily breakfast, dinner on select evenings, and a sunset cruise.

TOP ROMANTIC PASTIMES

- Listen to live reggae music at a local watering hole.

- Take a trot on horseback along one of the pictur-esque beaches.

- Relax at a thatched-roof beach bar, sipping mai tais and enjoying the surf.

- Share a slice of coconut that you plucked ripe from a tree.

Great Barrier Reef

AUSTRALIA

Reefer Madness

THE BIG PICTURE

You'll be holding hands as much on land as you will under water as you explore the Great Barrier Reef. The labyrinth of coral formations, together with hundreds of islands strewn across the sea, is one of Mother Nature's most prized creations. Romance and adventure, luxury and nature are the hallmarks of this unique destination.

BEST PLACES TO STAY

Dry off at night at the coral fringed **Orpheus Island Resort** *(T. 61.7.4777.7377, www.orpheus.com.au)*, an exclusive hideaway boasting its own national park. With a limit of only 42 guests and the absence of phones, television, and young children, the resort fosters intimacy. Disappear to the 16-villa **Voyages Bedarra Island** *(T. 61.2.8296. 8010, www. voyages.com.au)* off the Cairns coast. Get back to nature inside your luxurious rainforest villa with its separate living room, roomy bed, and inviting balcony.

TOP ROMANTIC PASTIMES

- Pack a picnic hamper and enjoy lunch while bobbing on a dinghy.
- Drape yourselves across massage tables at the beach for a couples' treatment.
- Enjoy the sapphire sea in a glass-bottom boat or catamaran.